Washi Style!

Washi Style!

Make it with paper tape

Over 101 Great Projects Using Japanese Style Decorative Tape

Marisa Edghill

ST. MARTIN'S GRIFFIN
NEW YORK

Washi Style

A Quarto Book

Copyright © 2015 by Quarto Inc.

All rights reserved.

Printed in China.

For information, address St. Martin's Press, 175 Fifth Avenue, New York, N.Y. 10010.

www.stmartins.com

Library of Congress Cataloging-in-Publication Data Available Upon Request

ISBN 978-1-250-05908-6

St. Martin's Griffin books may be purchased for educational, business, or promotional use. For information on bulk purchases, please contact Macmillan Corporate and Premium Sales Department at 1-800-221-7945, extension 5442, or write specialmarkets@macmillan.com.

First U.S. Edition: January 2015

10 9 8 7 6 5 4 3 2 1

Conceived, designed, and produced by
Quarto Publishing plc
The Old Brewery
6 Blundell Street
London N7 9BH

QUAR.WSMI

Project Editor: Chelsea Edwards
Art Editor: Jackie Palmer
Designer: Karin Skånberg
Photographers: Nicki Dowey (location) and Phil Wilkins (studio)
Illustrator: John Woodcock
Design Assistant: Martina Calvio
Copyeditor: Ruth Patrick
Proofreader: Sarah Hoggett
Indexer: Helen Snaith
Art Director: Caroline Guest
Creative Director: Moira Clinch
Publisher: Paul Carslake

Color separation in Singapore by Pica Digital Pte Limited

Printed in China
by 1010 Printing International Ltd

Contents

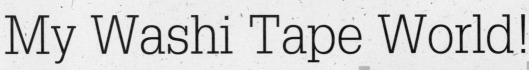

My Washi Tape World!

Wrap it, pleat it, collage it, stick it—once I started to play with washi tape, I was hooked and I think you will be too! You see, washi tape isn't just tape—use it well and it can also become a replacement for ribbon, pretty paper, or even paint.

My relationship with washi tape began in 2010 when I opened an online boutique full of all things cute, clever, and crafty. Japanese masking tape, which we now know as washi tape, was an instant bestseller and since then, it's been pretty much all washi, all the time around here. Creating with washi tape and inspiring others to try something new has become a big part of my business and rarely does a day go by

that I'm not up to my elbows in the stuff! Washi tape is well loved for its multi-tasking personality. Sticky, but not too sticky, it is repositionable, removable, oftentimes reusable, easy to tear, and provides a surface you can write on. Sounds pretty great, right? While the precedent for using washi tape seems to be stick a strip on it, within the pages of this book, you will learn to think beyond the strip and start using washi tape to its full potential.

love **Marisa**

I'd love to connect with you online, where I share my love for crafting with washi tape (oh, and other materials, too!) and plenty of DIY projects:

- Blog: www.omiyageblogs.ca
- Twitter: www.twitter.com/MarisaEdghill
- Facebook: www.facebook.com/Omiyage.ca
- Pinterest: www.pinterest.com/OmiyageCA
- Instagram: www.instagram.com/Omiyage_ca
- Shop: www.omiyage.ca

What Is Washi Tape?

Cute and colorful washi tape is the latest darling of the craft, design, and scrapbooking communities, but just what is it?

It's a bit difficult to pin down exactly what washi tape is without first discussing what it isn't. So let's start there. Washi tape isn't made of plastic (that's called deco tape). It isn't made of regular paper or tissue paper (that would be paper tape). And, despite what the Internet might be telling you, it can't be made at home.

Originally from Japan, washi tape is decorative tape made from special paper, which is strong yet delicate, with a low-tack adhesive. Its unique qualities make it easy to tear, position, and reposition on most surfaces, and also make it easy to write on.

Washi means Japanese paper (wa meaning "Japanese", shi meaning "paper"). The term itself is flexible, and can be understood as paper made using Japanese techniques and not specifically paper made in Japan. Each manufacturer uses its own unique washi tape "recipe", so you will find variations between different brands. Some are more translucent than others, some a little stickier. As you experiment with different tapes, you'll be sure to find some brands you like more than others.

QUALITIES OF WASHI TAPE

Tear, snip, stick, unstick, reposition, pleat, sew, and write—washi tape is a fantastic multitasker. Let's look at its best qualities.

Delicate but strong—Made from high-quality paper, washi tape is easy to tear by hand yet stronger than standard masking tape.

Flexible—The thin paper used to manufacture washi tape makes it perfect for use on many different surfaces and for both flat and wrapped applications.

Great for layering—As light-colored washi tape is slightly translucent, it's ideal for layering, allowing the color and texture of the surface below to peek through and add to the design.

Repositionable—The unique low-tack adhesive makes washi tape easy to remove and reposition on most surfaces. This makes it extremely easy to use (and reuse).

Archival quality—High-quality washi tape should be acid free and archival quality. It's a good idea to check that tapes meet these standards before using them for scrapbooking.

CONSTRAINTS OF WASHI TAPE

As with any material, there are some things you can't do with washi tape. When planning projects, it always helps to remember that it is a very pretty version of what is essentially a paper tape.

Don't mix tape and food—Do not apply tape to surfaces that will have direct contact with food or mouths. Some tapes have food safety clearance, but most do not. Washi tape looks wonderful when applied to the outside of a cup or the handle of a spoon, but keep tape away from areas that touch the lips or food.

Durability—Washi tape is not a permanent material. It looks great on your phone case or keyboard, but with prolonged use it is likely to look dirty and the edges will start to peel. For more information on extending the life of your washi tape, see page 13.

Strong but not that strong—The special paper used to make washi tape is known for being stronger than standard paper; however, the adhesive is not super sticky. While washi tape is great for decorating outgoing mail, it is not recommended for sealing boxes.

May damage some surfaces—While washi tape is easy to remove and reposition on many surfaces, it does occasionally catch and tear surfaces. It's always a good idea to check how your tape reacts to the desired surface in an inconspicuous area before committing.

Hot or wet surfaces—For safety's sake, don't apply washi tape directly to hot surfaces like light bulbs. To extend the life of your washi-taped vessels, don't soak them in water or place them in a dishwasher.

TYPES OF TAPE

From super-skinny ⅛-in.-wide (3 mm) tapes, all the way up to 8-in.-wide (20 cm) rolls, it seems there's a tape color, pattern, and size for pretty much any project you can dream up. Here's a look at some of the tape widths and designs used in this book.

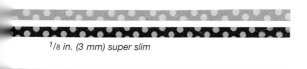

⅛ in. (3 mm) super slim

¼ in. (6–7 mm) slim pattern

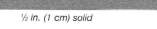

¼ in. (6–7 mm) slim solid

½ in. (1 cm) solid

⅝ in. (15 mm) standard width solid

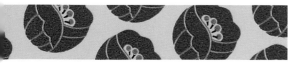

⅝ in. (15 mm) standard width pattern

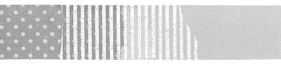

⅝ in. (15 mm) standard width multi-pattern

⅝ in. (15 mm) standard width stripe

¾ in. (2 cm) solid   *1¼ in. (3 cm) pattern*

Specialty tapes featuring photos or illustrations are so much fun to create with. They are also perfect for cutting into individual stickers.

Keep an eye out for die-cut tapes. Their shaped edges will add something new to your tape collection.

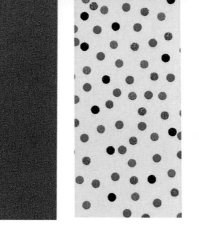

EDGE TREATMENTS

Don't just cut the tape straight across— experiment with different edge treatments.

Flat cut

Slanted cut

Ribbon cut

Rounded edge

Tape dispenser edge

Torn edge

Shaped with scissors

What is Washi Tape?   **9**

Washi Tape Basics

Washi tape may be super easy to use, but knowing a few basics will help you make the most of each roll. Use these tricks, tips, and techniques when crafting the projects in this book or to add your own washi style to everyday objects.

BEST SURFACES

Since washi tape is translucent, it looks best when it isn't competing with the material it's used on. Choose neutral or light-colored smooth surfaces like paper, wood, or glass. Try to avoid using tape on black or dark surfaces or anything with a prominent or uneven texture.

READY TO WASHI?

Simply stick strips of tape to the desired surface. Add a single accent strip or create a pattern with multiple pieces—there's no end to the options. You can tear or cut the tape or even carefully trim the edges with a craft knife once the tape is in position. Not in the right position? Gently peel the tape off and replace it in the desired spot. When wrapping tape around round surfaces, smooth out any wrinkles with your fingers.

PARCHMENT PAPER METHOD

Once you've mastered the washi tape strip, try creating shapes and pictures out of tape. To do so, you will need to apply strips of tape to waxed or parchment paper. Try to choose thicker paper and, when using waxed paper, apply the tape to the non-waxed side. The tape grabs onto the waxed surface and it's very difficult to remove. My favorite surface for creating shapes is actually the backing paper from labels— the glossy surface is perfect for use with washi tape, so if you use lots of labels at work, why not save the backing papers and try using them for some of these techniques?

Small shapes

While small shapes can be cut directly out of washi tape, it can get a bit frustrating as the tape sticks to both your fingers and scissors. Apply a strip of tape to waxed or parchment paper, then cut out the desired shapes with scissors or a craft knife. When you're ready to use the shapes, simply peel off the paper backing.

Pictures

Make collage-style pictures out of tape by breaking the image into sections. Use the multi-strip technique to create each individual section of the picture. It can help to trace a printout of a picture to keep the various pieces consistent in size and shape. Once all the pieces are ready, peel off the paper backings and assemble on the desired surface.

Multi-strip shapes and letters

To create larger shapes, overlap strips of tape on a piece of waxed or parchment paper. Work from one side to the other, applying strips one after another, ensuring each overlaps the one before it by a couple of millimeters. If desired, you can trace a shape or letter onto the waxed paper, then cover it in overlapping strips and cut out. Once the shape is cut out, carefully peel it off of the backing paper and stick it to the desired surface. Always peel from the bottommost piece of tape to keep your shape in one piece. This technique tends to be more effective when using patterned tapes, as the overlapped sections of tape are less obvious.

MAKING WASHI TAPE STICKERS

Creating stickers out of washi tape instantly increases its usefulness. Use stickers to make your own gift wrap, decorate envelopes, or in your craft projects. You can transform tape into pretty much any shape you please, here are three ideas to get you started.

Geometric Stickers

Simple shapes like squares, triangles, and diamonds are easily snipped right off of the roll. Cut straight across or at an angle to create the desired shape. Use the geometric shapes to create patterns or build pictures.

Specialty Stickers

Rolls of washi tape with individual pictures on are fantastic to have in your collection; not only do they look great, but they also are easily made into stickers. Apply the tape to parchment or waxed paper. Cut around the outside edges of the pictures. To use, peel off of the paper backing and stick.

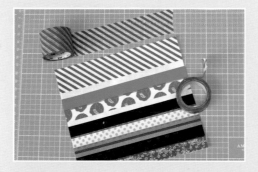

Dot Stickers

1. Apply strips of washi tape to a piece of waxed or parchment paper. Use a wide tape, overlap standard strips, or create a pattern with a variety of different designs. Make sure that the edges of the tape overlap slightly.

2. Flip the paper over and use your roll of tape as a template to draw circles. Use scissors to cut out the stickers. Alternatively, you can use a circle punch, though most punches have a hard time with waxed paper. Peel off of the paper backing to use.

Working With Washi Tape

To make the most of washi tape, it sometimes helps to think of it as more than just tape. When you allow it to take the place of paint, ribbon, or fabric, suddenly the options for how to use it seem almost endless. Here are a few techniques to try.

LAYERING

Since washi tape is slightly translucent, you can create really lovely effects by layering different colors and patterns. Try creating a collage-style effect or layer longer strips for an all-over pattern.

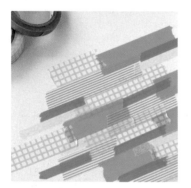 

1. Tear a short strip of washi tape and apply to the desired surface. Continue tearing and applying strips of various colors, designs, and lengths, allowing the ends and edges to overlap slightly.

2. Apply one long strip of tape all the way across your working surface. Apply a second strip at a 90-degree angle to the first. Continue layering long strips of tape at different angles until the desired pattern is created.

PLEATING

Add another dimension to your projects by pleating the tape. You can either pleat in a straight line or in the round. With this technique, you should work with tape on the roll.

1. Stick the first ⅝ in. (1.5 cm) of tape to the desired surface. Fold the tape back on itself, covering approximately half of the tape below. Secure the pleat by sticking the next ¼ in. (6–7 mm) to your working surface. From the edge of the first pleat to the point where you will start the second should be about ⅝ in. (1.5 cm). Continue pleating until the desired length is achieved.

2. The easiest way to pleat in the round is to create your pleats around the circumference of a circular shape. Attach the tape to the circle so that about one-third of the tape is on the paper and the other two-thirds hangs over the edge. Pleat around the circle, turning the circle shape as you go. When you have finished pleating, cut the tape and hide the end under the first pleat.

WEAVING

Take the layering of tape one step further by actually weaving pieces of tape. To best showcase this technique, choose two or four different tapes.

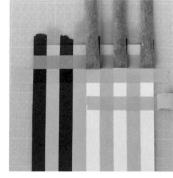

1. Apply evenly spaced strips of tape that run from the top edge to the bottom edge of the desired surface

2. Apply one horizontal strip of tape across the vertical strips. Then add a second set of strips in each of the vertical spaces.

3. Lift the first set of vertical strips, peeling back to the position of the first horizontal piece of tape. Apply a second piece of tape horizontally directly below the first. Replace the lifted strips.

4. Continue weaving the tape by lifting and then replacing the strips of tape in a standard over-under basketweave pattern.

APPLYING WASHI TAPE TO WALLS

Whether you want to create a wall of stripes, a fun mural for a kid's room, or a unique party decoration, washi tape is a great material for dressing up a blank wall. Before applying tape to your wall, make sure that it won't damage the surface—if there are uneven patches or chips in the paint, the tape is likely to pull off some paint when you remove it. Before committing to a large tape installation, it's a good idea to test the tape in a small inconspicuous spot. When creating pictures, you can either tear and apply strips as you go or use a craft knife and ruler to create more precise edges right on the wall. When using a craft knife to cut tape on your wall, use a light touch. You want to cut just the tape without cutting through it and damaging the wall surface below.

SEWING WASHI TAPE

When sewing washi tape, there are a couple of things to remember. It's always a good idea to have a needle dedicated to sewing paper, as this dulls the needle point. Also, the adhesive from washi tape can build up on your needle and slow things down. Have a couple of pieces of scrap fabric on hand, and when the machine starts to feel sluggish, run them through the machine a couple of times to clean off any adhesive. It is good practice to sew a couple of lines on the scrap fabric to clean the needle between each washi tape project.

WRITING ON TAPE

While washi tape makes great labels and gift tags, not all pens work on its unique surface. Choose a ballpoint pen or a permanent marker, as most liquid ink pens will smear.

MAKE IT PERMANENT

To extend the life of your washi tape projects, it's a great idea to add a coating. This is particularly useful for items that will be handled a lot. For most coated items in this book, I've used découpage glue, which is a glue and sealant in one. You can choose a matte or glossy finish to match your preferences. For extra protection on items such as furniture, or items that are likely to have contact with liquids, choose a waterproof acrylic sealant that can be brushed or sprayed on.

It can take a little trial and error to find the perfect pen or marker for writing on washi tape. Fine-tip permanent markers are my personal favorite.

Wishing you a happy birthday

Washi Tape Projects

You might be asking yourself, "What can I do with washi tape?" Well, grab a few rolls and get ready to be inspired. From cute greetings cards to useful housewares to lovely pieces of jewelry, there's a project here for everyone. Delve into this treasury of unique projects and soon you'll be asking yourself, "What *can't* I do with washi tape?"

GREETINGS

Learn how to create unique handmade cards and envelopes for any occasion. Cute birthday cards, clever shaped cards, and decorative envelopes will inspire you to send more mail. With a variety of techniques and ideas to try, you'll never need to buy a boring drugstore card again.

Making your own cards and sending snail mail doesn't have to be complicated. These ideas will have you crafting up cute cards and sending off pretty mail in just a few minutes.

Colorful envelopes

An envelope makes a great canvas for trying out all sorts of washi tape techniques. Seal with a strip or two of tape, decorate with colorful washi tape dot stickers, add a touch of whimsy with a striped flap, or even outline the entire envelope with tape. No matter which design you choose, your envelopes will look fantastic.

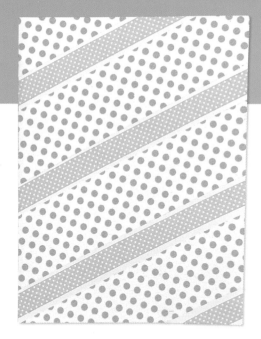

Quick cards

When you're looking for something sweet but simple, try adding ribbon strips, a classic heart shape, or stripes to the front of a blank card. Whip up one in a hurry or craft up a stack at once. You'll never be caught without a card again.

Cute index cards

Sometimes a simple note is all you need—perhaps a folded card feels too formal or you just want to slip a sweet message into a loved one's lunchbox. Add a few strips of tape to a standard index card and you've got a notecard worth taking notice of.

Birthday Cards

Everyone loves a handmade card. These cute cards are easy to make and full of birthday fun. Colorful gifts and festive party hats are appropriate for all ages; simply choose different colors and patterns to match each recipient.

Birthday gift card

Start by creating a washi tape square. Apply strips of washi tape to parchment or waxed paper until the desired size is achieved. Be sure to slightly overlap each piece of tape with the one before it. Cut the tape-covered paper into a square or rectangle. Carefully peel the tape shape off of the paper backing, starting with the bottommost strip, and stick to the front of your blank card. Add a vertical strip of tape up the center of the square to resemble ribbon. Create a bow out of tape strips. For even more birthday fun, make a card with three small presents rather than one big one.

Party hats card

To create the triangles, apply strips of washi tape to parchment or waxed paper until the desired size is achieved. Be sure to slightly overlap each piece of tape with the one before it. Cut the tape-covered paper into three triangles. Carefully peel the tape shapes off the paper backing, starting with the bottommost strip, and stick to the front of your blank card. Make pom-poms for the tops of the hats by tearing four short strips of super-slim tape and overlapping in a star shape.

◀ Why not make a card with one large party hat rather than three small ones? The extra space gives you plenty of room to decorate.

Thank-you Cards

Show the world you have impeccable manners by sending a handcrafted thank-you card. Of course, you don't need to limit yourself to words of thanks—once you've mastered the skill of crafting washi tape letters, you can spell out anything you please!

1. Apply two strips of standard-width ⅝-in. (15-mm) washi tape to a piece of parchment or waxed paper. Make sure you slightly overlap the pieces of tape.

2. Cut out the tape-covered piece of paper. Trim to approximately 2 in. (5 cm) shorter than the width of the card. Cut the resulting length into the same number of pieces as the desired number of letters.

3. Cut out the required letters. I prefer to cut letters freehand; however, if you are more comfortable cutting from an outline, refer to the tracing instructions on page 37.

4. Lay out the letters on the front of your card to determine the placement and spacing. One letter at a time, peel the tape letters from the paper backing, making sure to start from the bottommost tape strip, and stick them to the card. I find it easiest to start by applying the first and last letters, then to fill in the middle.

Cut letters to the approximate size before shaping begins.

Tip: Apply a piece of washi tape across the width of your blank card. Use it as a straight-edge reference as you apply your letters. Once all letters are in place, carefully peel off the tape strip and discard.

Layer Cake Cards

Feeling a little bit fancy? It's time to build your dream cake, out of tape! I am of the opinion that washi tape is perfectly suited for creating beautiful layer cakes. Sure, you can't eat them, but you can use them to spread good cheer for all sorts of occasions. After all, who doesn't enjoy the sight of a really great cake?

You will need:

- Blank card—instructions based on standard 6 x 4-in. (A6) card
- Washi tape
- Scissors
- Craft knife (optional)
- Metallic gel pen (optional)

1. Start by building the basic layers of your cake. For the bottom layer, cut a piece of tape approximately 2½ in. (6 cm) long. Apply to the card about 2¾ in. (7 cm) from the bottom edge. Make sure the strip is positioned in the center of the card. Next, create the middle layer by cutting a strip of tape approximately 1¾ in. (4.5 cm) long. Apply on top of the bottom layer, leaving a small gap between the two strips of tape. Finally, add a 1¼-in. (3-cm) strip on top of the middle layer, leaving a small gap between the two strips.

2. Next, you are going to create the cake stand. Apply a slim piece of washi tape below the bottom layer of the cake. You want the ends of the slim tape to extend beyond the edges of cake by about ¼ in. (6 mm) on each side. Apply a second shorter strip of the slim tape about 1 in. (2.5 cm) below the strip you just laid to create the base. Fill in the space with a simple vertical strip or add more detail with shaped strips as in the example cards (see left).

3. Decorate your cake with delicate washi tape details or doodle classic cake designs onto your cake with a metallic pen. If desired, add a simple—or not so simple—cake topper. Once you've built the basic cake, the details are really up to you. A craft knife can come in handy at this point if you are applying washi tape details. Use the knife to carefully trim any tape ends that extend beyond the sides of the cake. Don't press too hard, since you only want to cut through a thin piece of tape.

Delicious Donut Cards

Break with the standard rectangular card and make something more delicious. Clever donut-shaped cards are the perfect greeting for any occasion. Once you get the hang of creating this shaped card, you can make cards in any shape you please.

You will need:
- Cream card stock 8½ x 11 in. (A4)
- Scissors
- Parchment or waxed paper
- Washi tape
- Craft knife (optional)

1. Fold the card stock in half vertically. Draw an approximately 4 in. (10 cm) circle on the card stock—one side of the circle should slightly overlap the folded edge. To create the circle, try drawing around a bowl or other round object. Cut out the circle.

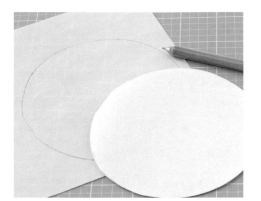

2. Draw the same size circle on a piece of parchment or waxed paper. To create the frosting shape out of tape, cover the parchment paper circle with overlapping strips of washi tape. Shape the frosting by cutting slightly inside the line and creating an uneven wavy edge as you cut.

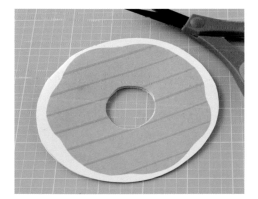
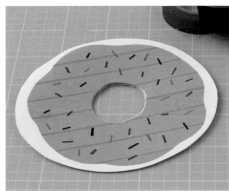

3. Starting with the bottommost strip of tape, carefully peel the frosting shape off the parchment paper and stick to the center front of the card. Cut an approximately 1½ in. (4 cm) circle in the center of the card with scissors or a craft knife.

4. Garnish your donut with washi tape sprinkles. Cut very thin strips of tape, then cut each thin strip into thirds (about ⅛ in. [3 mm] long), and apply randomly to the frosting portion of your card.

◀ The finished cards look good enough to eat and are a sweet way to invite someone over for tea!

Whether you're looking to wish someone you love a happy new home or just to reach out and say hello, these cute cottage cards are a wonderful way to do it. With washi tape and card stock, you can create custom cards in virtually any shape you please.

Tip: When covering your cottage with tape, it's easier to tear strips off the roll as you go. After all the tape is placed, trim any excess from the edges with a pair of scissors.

Cute Cottage Cards

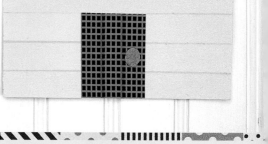

1. Using a standard 8½ x 11-in. (A4) piece of card stock, you can make two cards. Fold the card stock in half horizontally and crease firmly. A bone folder can be helpful in getting nice sharp folds, but isn't necessary. Cut the card stock in half. You will be left with two cards 5½ in. wide x 4¼ in. tall (14 x 11.5 cm).

2. Using the template on page 125, trace the shape of the house onto the card. Don't forget the chimney!

3. Start by covering the roof in the desired washi tape. Carefully trim the excess tape away from the chimney using a craft knife. Be careful not to cut through the card stock. Cover the chimney in a contrasting washi tape design.

4. Cut out the roof and chimney with scissors. If desired, cover the walls of the house in washi tape—the cottages also look cute with white walls.

5. Use three strips of tape to build a door. Finally, add a circular doorknob.

Simple Holiday Cards

Sometimes simple is better. Make a pile of these quick-and-easy Christmas tree cards to send to your entire mailing list this holiday season. And while you're at it, why not make it a family affair? While the cards are designed with you in mind, kids of all ages will have fun crafting trees out of tape while older kids will master the star toppers with ease.

1. Tear four strips of washi tape, each slightly shorter than the one before. Starting with the longest strip and, working your way upward, apply the four strips to the front of your blank card. Ensure that each strip is evenly spaced and centered.

2. To create the trunk of your Christmas tree, tear a short piece of washi tape in a contrasting color. Be sure to center the trunk below the lowest tree strip.

3. To make the star topper, start by applying two short strips of the desired washi tape to a piece of parchment or waxed paper, overlapping them slightly. Cut the square of tape-covered paper out of the larger piece of paper. Flip it over and sketch a simple star. Cut it out. Carefully peel the tape off the paper, starting with the bottommost piece of tape. Stick the star to your card at the top of the tree.

↑ For extra impact, try outlining the edges of your envelope with tape strips. For more decorative envelope ideas, turn to page 28.

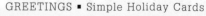

Garland Cards

In this project, two fun ideas combine into one fantastic card. A simple confetti-inspired card is sure to delight when the recipient opens it up to discover a garland on the inside. Perfect for celebrating birthdays or congratulating someone. Looking for a simpler card project? Skip the garland and just decorate the exterior of the card.

Tip: If you are having trouble getting your garland flags to sit flat, try taping the piece of twine to your work surface. Keep the twine taut as you add each tape flag.

You will need:

- Blank card—instructions based on standard 6 x 4-in. (A6) size card
- Washi tape
- Scissors
- Fine permanent marker (optional)
- Twine or string

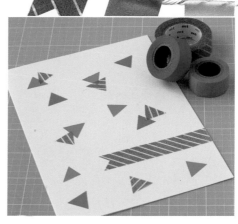

1. Cut a ribbon notch in one end of a strip of washi tape. Apply to the front of the blank card. Trim the end of the tape so that it is flush with the edge of the card. If desired, use a fine permanent marker to write a short message on the strip of tape.

2. Cut small triangles of tape and apply randomly to the front of the card to create a confetti-like pattern. Use different widths of tape to make different sizes of triangles. Try overlapping a few triangles to give the pattern more depth.

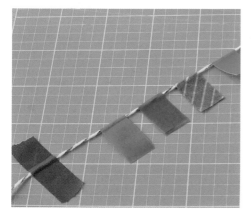

3. Next, create the small garland for the inside of the card. Start with a piece of twine or string approximately 12–13 in. (30–33 cm) long. Tear off a piece of washi tape approximately 2 in. (5 cm) long. Make your first flag about 2 in. (5 cm) from one end of the twine. Place the twine in the center of the strip of tape and fold the two sides of the tape together.

4. Continue adding flags until the garland is approximately 8 in. (20.5 cm) long. Trim the flags to a uniform length. Shape the strips into flags by cutting a triangular notch in each one.

5. Use two small strips of washi tape to attach the garland to the upper corners of the inside of the card.

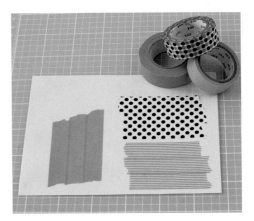

1. First decide whether to create your design by cutting freehand or by drawing. If you prefer to work from a picture, draw onto the parchment or waxed paper before adding the washi tape. Simple shapes work best. Cover the desired area with overlapping strips of washi tape.

You will need:
- Blank envelopes
- Parchment or waxed paper
- Washi tape
- Scissors
- Metallic pen or fine permanent marker (optional)

Decorative Envelopes

Make someone's day by sending them a piece of pretty mail. While we pay lots of attention to greeting cards, the average envelope gets neglected. When you send a decorated envelope in the mail, it spreads joy to everyone who handles it along the way. You can decorate your envelope to match the card inside or craft up a totally different theme.

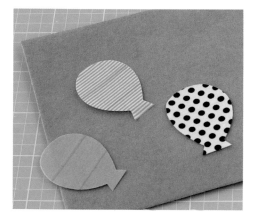 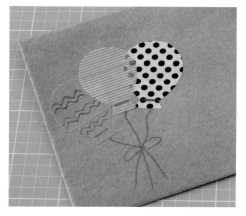 

2. Cut out the tape shapes. Starting from the bottommost strip of tape, carefully peel the shapes off the paper background and apply to the envelope. Be sure to leave space for the mailing address and stamps.

3. If desired, use a fine permanent marker or metallic pen to add details to your picture. Check to make sure your chosen marker/pen is compatible with writing on washi tape—smears on your finished work are simply no fun.

4. Don't forget the back of the envelope. Create a small picture or add some interest with a strip or two of tape.

◀ Match your envelope to the occasion—try balloons for birthdays, presents for Christmas, or hearts for Valentine's Day.

WRAPPING

Gifts wrapped with washi tape are wrapped in style! Decorate simple gift bags, craft one-of-a-kind tags, or learn how to make your own wrapping paper and bows. From simple 5-minute ideas to more complex multi-step projects, you'll be sure to have the best-wrapped gift at the party.

Quick Starts

With washi tape in your craft cupboard, pretty gift-wrapping solutions are right at your fingertips. Dress up basic paper bags, shipping tags, and small boxes in just a few steps.

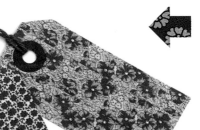

Gift tags

Plain shipping tags are easily upgraded with washi tape and some clever trimming. Cover the entire tag with strips of washi tape, making sure not to leave any spaces between the strips. Trim the excess tape from the edges. Then, carefully cut around the reinforcing ring with a craft knife and discard the circle of extra tape.

Pillow boxes

Pillow boxes are the perfect size for wrapping up small gifts. Layer two tape designs on top of each other to mimic the look of ribbon. Don't have a wide roll? Not to worry, simply apply two strips of the same tape next to each other before topping with the second design.

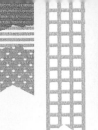

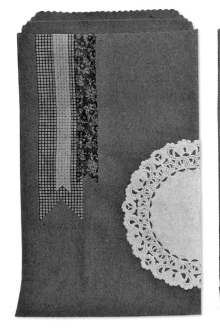

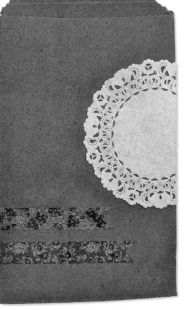

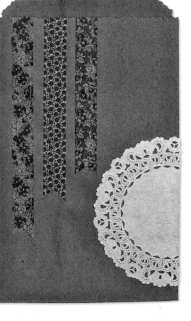

Colored bags sealed with tape

Seal paper bags with a strip or two of tape. Notched ends and a washi tape sticker take this quick wrapping idea from simple to sensational.

Brown gift bags and doilies

Brown gift bags, washi tape, and paper doilies make a wonderful combination. Try different combinations of patterns, colors, and widths. For less mess and easy repositioning, use a spray adhesive when working with paper doilies.

Need a gift tag in a hurry? These simple geometric tags look great alone and even better layered. Plus, no fancy techniques are necessary—simply stick, snip, and sign.

Layered Gift Tags

1. Cover a piece of neutral-colored card stock with strips of washi tape. When laying strips next to each other, be sure to match up the pattern where possible.

2. Punch or cut a variety of circles, squares, and notched ribbon shapes. Use a small hole punch to create a hole in each shape for twine or ribbon.

3. Tie one onto your gift, or for a more dynamic look, layer a mix of different sizes, colors, and shapes.

with love from me x

Need some blank space to write? Just apply a single strip of washi tape to your card stock before cutting or punching out shapes.

One of my favorite things about washi tape is its versatility, especially when it comes to wrapping gifts. There are so many ways to incorporate washi tape into gift wrap, but it really shines when you use it with plain white paper. Here are three easy ways to make spectacular-looking gifts.

Washi tape ribbon

Three Ways to Wrap with Washi Tape

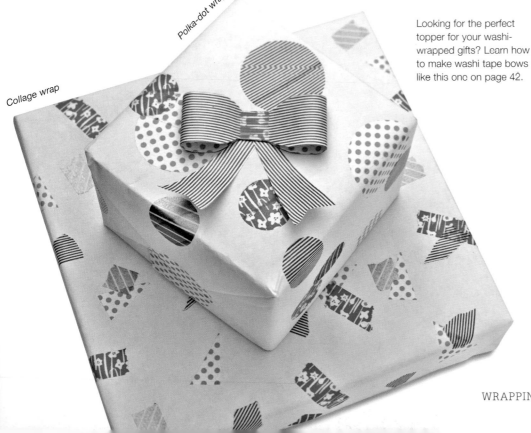

Polka-dot wrap

Collage wrap

Looking for the perfect topper for your washi-wrapped gifts? Learn how to make washi tape bows like this one on page 42.

Washi tape ribbon
Wrap strips of washi tape around the wrapped box. Keep it simple with a single strip or layer different colors and widths. To create the illusion of really wide ribbon, as in the example above, apply two stripes of wide washi tape to the box with a slight gap between them. Then apply another design of wide washi tape over the gap. Finally, top with a third slimmer tape design.

Polka-dot wrap
Make washi tape dot stickers in a variety of sizes and colors, using the tape dots technique described on page 11. Apply randomly to all sides of your wrapped box. For added interest, be sure to overlap some of the dots.

Collage wrap
This quick decorative technique is also a fun one. Create your own collage-style wrapping paper by applying a variety of different washi tape shapes to all sides of the box. Try a mix of triangles, torn strips, and shapes in different sizes and patterns. Don't think too much about composition—the final wrap design should look random, not symmetrical.

Confetti Bows

Looking for a unique gift topper? Look no further! Clever confetti bows are a super-quick project, but are a fun way to make any parcel look sensational. Customize each bow by choosing different confetti materials and washi tape colors.

1

2

Don't feel limited to sequins or spangles—you can fill your confetti bows with any small and light material you choose. Try tissue paper shapes, paper confetti, or even dried flower petals.

1. To make a confetti bow, start with a clear, flat bag. Any size will do—the bigger the bag, the bigger the bow. Fill the bag with a few pinches of the desired confetti material. Fold a strip of washi tape over the open end of the bag to seal it. Repeat on the opposite side of the bag. Trim the tape edges, being careful not to cut the bag.

2. Distribute the confetti evenly between the two sides of the bag. Pinch the center of the bag to create a bow shape and wrap a strip of washi tape around the center. Shape the bow with your fingers. Use transparent sticky tape to attach the bow to the top of your present.

Monogrammed Gift Topper

Simple and striking washi tape monograms not only look great—they also mean you can skip the gift tag! Choose different washi tape colors and patterns to suit the recipient—this is one packaging style that suits everyone. Once you've mastered the technique for creating large washi tape letters, you can use them to customize blank notebooks, greetings cards, or even to create art.

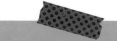

You will need:

- Mirror printout of desired letter
- Parchment or waxed paper
- Washi tape
- Marker or pen in a dark color
- Scissors

Washi tape letters and twine tassels make a great pair. Turn to pages 86–87 for instructions on crafting your own tassels.

1. Print out the mirror image of the desired letter. Try to choose a font size to match the size of your parcel. Cut out the letter, leaving a rectangular border around it.

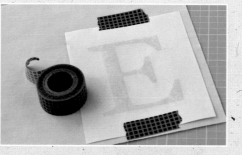

2. Place the printout face down on the right side of the parchment or waxed paper. Secure in place with two short strips of tape.

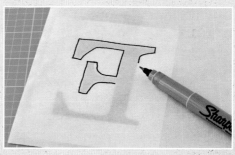

3. Flip the paper over and trace the outline with a dark marker or pen. You want to make sure that you can see the lines through the parchment or waxed paper.

4. Flip the paper back over and remove the printout. Starting at the bottom apply strips of washi tape, making sure that each strip slightly overlaps the one before it.

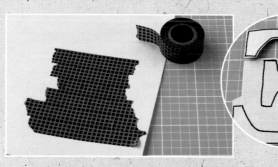

5. Once the letter is covered with tape, flip the paper over again and use the letter outline as a cutting guide. Cut slightly outside the lines to give the final letter more impact.

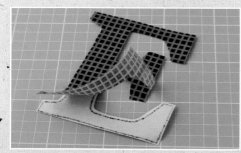

6. Starting from the bottommost strip of tape, carefully peel the tape letter off the paper backing.

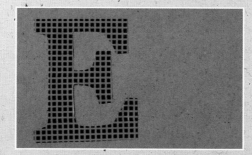

7. Apply to the top of your gift, smoothing out any wrinkles.

Rosette Ribbons

Here washi tape replaces ribbon to create fun sticky-backed rosette or award ribbons. The pleating technique can be a little tricky, but once you've got the hang of it you'll be dreaming up occasions worthy of an award!

You will need:
- Card stock in a neutral color
- Scissors
- Washi tape
- Glue stick (optional)
- Circle punch (optional)

Mix and match different colors, patterns, and sizes of tape for a unique modern version or craft them out of traditional blue, red, and yellow for use in an impromptu award ceremony. These ribbons make wonderful gift toppers and can double as gift tags—just write your message in the center. Attach one to the front of a blank card for a new take on the badge birthday card. Or why not use them as nametags for your next event?

1. For each rosette, cut or punch a circle out of the card stock. For a small rosette, you will need a 1-in. (2.5-cm) circle. For a large rosette, you will need a 2-in. (5-cm) circle. Stick the loose end of the washi tape to the circle so that about one third of the width of the tape is on the circle and the rest hangs over the edge. Make a fold in the tape, creating your first pleat (see page 12 for pleating tips). Make even pleats all the way around the circle. Do not tear or cut the tape until you have finished the entire circle.

2. When you have pleated all the way around the circle, cut the tape and tuck the loose end under the first pleat for a seamless look. To create the center of your rosette, punch or cut a circle from washi tape-covered card stock. The circle should be the same size as your original circle. Attach the tape-covered circle to the center of the rosette with glue or tape.

Tip: If you would like more ruffles on your rosette, try adding a second layer of pleated tape before attaching the center circle.

3. To make the ribbon strips, apply two pieces of washi tape approximately 4 in. (10 cm) long to another piece of the card stock. Cut out these strips and create a V-shaped notch at one end of each. Flip your rosette over and attach the ribbon strips to the back with a piece of tape or glue, adjusting the length and angle of the strips before securing.

Indulge your sweet tooth with these sugar-free gift tags. With washi tape, you can craft a gift tag in the form of any simple picture using a few strips of tape and some clever cutting. Get inspired by these tasty versions of donuts, ice-cream cones, and cupcakes, and then craft your own adorable treats.

Cute Shaped Gift Tags

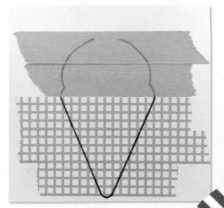

◀ Templates for these tags are provided on page 124. Copy the templates onto card stock or use the shapes as a jumping-off point for creating your own cute tags.

Donuts

The easiest way to create donut tags is with circle punches. Alternatively, you can use the template on page 124. Cut or punch a 2-in. (5-cm) circle out of card stock. To make the frosting, trace the punched circle onto a piece of parchment or waxed paper. Cover with overlapping strips of washi tape. Cut out the circle, creating a wavy edge on the inside of your traced line. Peel the frosting shape off the paper and stick to the card stock circle. Cut a smaller circle in the center of the donut shape. Create sprinkles by cutting slivers of tape. For more details on creating washi tape donuts, see page 22.

Ice-cream cones

The trick to creating an ice-cream cone shape is to imagine a long triangle topped with a semicircle. It's easiest to build your cone on a small piece of card stock and then cut it out. Cover the cone section with one color of washi tape and the ice-cream section with another. Top with a small circle to represent a cherry. Cut out your tag. Punch a hole in the cherry for your string or ribbon.

Cupcakes

Making cupcakes is quite similar to ice cream—at least when it comes to tags. Cover the top half of the cupcake shape with one color of washi tape and the bottom half with another. Don't forget the sprinkles! Cut out your shape, punch a small hole, and string onto ribbon or twine.

1. Start with a standard piece of 8½ x 11-in. (A4) printer paper. Cut off a lengthwise strip approximately 1¼ in. (3 cm) wide. Set aside.

Washi Tape Bows

Every gift deserves a fantastic topper. While washi tape makes a great substitute for ribbon when wrapping gifts, it can be frustrating to find a matching bow. Once you know how to craft your own adorable bows out of washi tape and paper, you'll never be frustrated again… and your gifts will be the best dressed in the room!

You will need:
- Standard printer paper
- Washi tape—preferably two designs 1¼ in. (30 mm) wide and one ⅝ in. (15 mm) wide
- Scissors

5. Ensuring that the desired tape design is on the outside, make your tape-covered piece of paper into a loop, overlapping the paper ends by approximately ½ in. (1 cm) and using the extra piece of tape extending from the one end to secure.

Tip: Want to make a washi tape bow but don't have 1¼-in. (30-mm) wide tape on hand? No problem! Simply use two strips of standard ⅝ in. (15 mm) wide washi tape in place of the wide tape. Make sure there are no gaps between the strips of tape and try to match up the pattern where possible. You can see this technique used in step two for the inside of the bow.

9. Apply a strip of washi tape approximately 3 in. (7.5 cm) long to the paper strip you set aside in step one. Cut out.

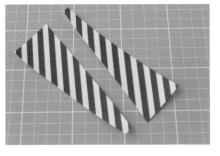

10. Cut the strip lengthwise into two triangular shapes with flat points

2. Choose a wide washi tape design for the inside of your bow. Lay a strip of this tape along the bottom edge of the paper. Trim any excess tape ends from the paper edges.

3. Flip the paper over. Choose a wide washi tape design for the outside of your bow. Lay a strip of the tape along the bottom edge of the paper, allowing ½ in. (1 cm) of the tape to extend past one of the sides of the paper.

4. Cut out the tape-covered strip of paper.

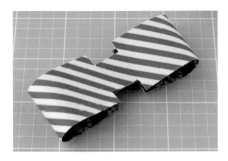

6. Flatten the loop slightly without creasing. Be sure to keep the connecting seam at the center back. Cut a notch approximately ⅝ in. (1.5 cm) wide by ¼ in. (6 mm) deep in the center of each side of the bow.

7. Wrap a piece of standard width ⅝-in. (15-mm) washi tape around the center of the bow to secure.

8. Trim the four edges of the center of the bow, rounding them with your scissors.

11. Cut notches into the bottoms of each of the triangular shapes to create ribbons.

12. Secure the ribbon strips to the back of your bow with a piece of tape.

Striped Gift Bags

One of my favorite things about washi tape is that you really don't have to be artistic to use it. These striped gift bags are a great example of that. Simply add a few strips of washi tape to a plain bag and you have one-of-a-kind wrapping you'll be proud to gift.

Ribbon stripes

Vertical strips of washi tape take on the appearance of ribbon when you add a notch to the end of each strip. Before you start, make sure that the end of your washi tape is a straight cut, not a torn edge. Cut a triangular notch into the end of your tape. Place the notched end of the tape on the bag and run the tape strip all the way up to the upper edge of the bag. Cut the tape, making sure that the tape lines up with the bag edge. Apply more tape strips, varying the lengths for more interest.

Horizontal stripes

Turn a plain gift bag into a festive striped bag using washi tape strips. Apply tape strips all the way across the width of the bag. No need to be neat at this point; simply tear the ends, leaving a little overlap over the edges of the bag. Once all the tape strips have been placed, trim the edges. Try mixing and matching different widths and colors of tape. Watch your spacing, and remember that the blank space becomes stripes too.

Abstract stripes

Ready for a little fun? Start by applying one tape strip across the bag at an angle. Then add a second strip at a different angle. Make sure that the two strips intersect, with the second strip overlapping the first. Continue adding strips, varying the angles and intersection points, until you are satisfied.

Don't forget to accessorize! Use a rosette ribbon as a gift tag. Turn to page 38 for instructions.

XOXO

Spell it out! Write a message on the front of the gift bag using washi tape letters. You can either build letters out of tape strips like the Xs, or cut letters from tape-covered parchment or waxed paper like the Os. For more tips on creating washi tape letters, turn to page 36.

Hearts

Apply overlapping strips of washi tape to a piece of parchment or waxed paper. Fold the tape-covered paper in half and cut a large heart shape. Then, with the paper still folded, use the outside edge of the heart as a guide to cut a smaller heart inside the larger heart. The width of the outer heart outline should be about ½ in. (1 cm). Repeat this process inside the smaller heart. Peel the first shape off the backing and stick to the bag. Repeat with the second. If desired, add a smaller heart in a contrasting color.

Ribbon

A pretty bow is the perfect accessory for any occasion. Start by applying a strip of tape from the top to the bottom of the bag. Then build your bow using the parchment or waxed paper shape technique (see pages 10–11). For the bow, you will need two rounded triangles, two ribbon strips with notched ends, and a center oval. Determine the position of your bow, apply the two ribbon strips, then place the rounded triangles so that the narrow ends face each other, and finish with the center oval.

Festive Gift Bags

A plain gift bag makes a great blank canvas. Whatever the occasion, washi tape is a simple way to customize basic gift bags into something special. These examples were inspired by Valentine's Day, but you could adapt the idea to another festivity.

Tip: A little washi tape goes a long way on a gift tag. Decorate blank gift tags to match your bags using stripes or small cutouts.

Make Your Own Washi Tape Wrap

Ever wanted to design your own wrapping paper? With this project, you'll be able to create all sorts of designs without even leaving your home office. Plus, by copying your design on your all-in-one printer or a color copier, you can replicate it over and over again without using up all of your washi tape. Wrapping paper created on regular printer paper is the perfect size for wrapping up small boxes; alternatively, join multiple pages and designs together for a fun patchwork look.

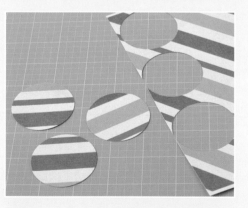

Tip: Once you've finished making copies, carefully peel the tape off the paper. Because washi tape is removable and can be repositioned on most surfaces, you should be able to reuse the tape from one wrap design to make another.

You will need:
- Standard printer paper
- Washi tape
- Scissors
- Home printer with color copy capability or access to a color photocopier

1. Starting with a blank piece of paper, use washi tape strips and shapes to create a pattern. Try striped designs or create confetti-inspired patterns using small triangles, squares, or circles.

2. Make color copies of your wrapping paper design on your home printer or a color copier. Use to wrap small gifts or for other paper crafts such as crafting your own envelopes.

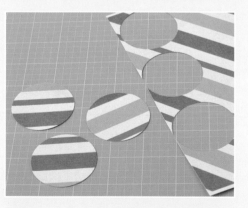

3. While you're at it, why not make matching gift tags by copying your design onto card stock. Then punch or cut out the desired tag shape.

CELEBRATIONS

Add some festive flavor to your next party or favorite holiday with cute and colorful washi tape party favors and decorations. Impress your guests with customized party décor, let washi tape help set the table for dinner parties, or even create your very own Christmas tree.

Quick Starts

Add some washi style to your next party with a few simple details. While these ideas take just a few minutes, the extra attention to detail won't be overlooked.

Cupcake Flags
For a sweet finishing touch for cupcakes and other treats, fold strips of washi tape over toothpicks and trim the ends into the desired shape. Straight, notched, or pointed, these flags are real cuties.

Party Cups
Washi tape allows you to put away the good glasses and embrace the paper or plastic cup. A few strips and stripes around the cup add tons of fun. Even better, leave a pile of washi tape next to the blank cups and let your guests add their own flair.

Favor Boxes
Classic mini takeout boxes make a striking addition to your candy buffet when decorated with a little (or a lot) of colorful washi tape. Add some color and pattern to each with a mix of stripes and shapes.

Sweet Spoons
Add some flair to sweet wooden dessert spoons. Try a few strips of washi wrapped around the handle or cover with a single strip. Just make sure to keep the tape away from the bowl of the spoon—no one wants a mouthful of tape with their ice cream sundae!

Ruffled place cards make a fanciful addition to any dinner party. With their unique pleated washi tape flourishes, these look wonderful at each place setting or as labels for the buffet. Your guests are sure to be impressed by your attention to detail.

Ruffled Place Cards

1. Start with store-bought cards or create your own out of card stock. To make your own, simply fold a piece of 3½ x 5-in. (9 x 13-cm) card stock in half. Make sure to use a bone folder for a nice crisp fold.

2. Start the ruffle at the bottom left edge of the card. Allow the end of the tape to extend slightly past the bottom edge, securing the card in place on your work surface.

3. Pleat the washi tape all the way up the left side of the card. Each pleat should be about ¼ in. (6 mm) long. Once you reach the top, you can either cut the tape off at the top edge or run the tape along the back to the bottom edge. No need to pleat the back.

4. Trim the tape ends so that they are flush with the card. For an optional finishing touch, sew a straight line of stitching down the center of your washi tape ruffle.

Tip: Is all this talk of pleats and stitching making you sweat? Make a simpler version by applying straight strips of the desired washi tapes to the left edge of the cards. Mix and match different colors and patterns for a more dynamic look.

Quick and Easy Napkin Rings

For a casual affair, a simple paper napkin is all you need, but, if we're being honest, they can also be kind of boring. Add a touch of fun and function with colorful washi tape napkin rings. Use a single tape design or embrace the philosophy of more is more, at least when it comes to tape, and combine different patterns and widths of tape.

1. Cut a standard piece of printer paper in half lengthwise. You'll be laying strips of tape across the width of the paper. For the bottommost layer of tape, you'll want to use wide 1¼-in. (30 mm) washi tape or apply two strips of standard-width tape next to each other. Allow one end of the tape to extend past the edge of the paper by approximately ½ in. (1 cm). Cut the other side so that it is flush with the paper edge.

2. Layer different widths and patterns of tape on top of one another to create your favorite combination.

3. Cut along the edges of the tape so that no plain paper is visible. Roll your napkin, then wrap the napkin ring around the napkin, securing with the loose tape end.

Having friends over for a sushi feast? Craft up these clever handmade chopstick cases. Some simple folds and a few decorative strips are all you need to add a little wow to the dinner table. Slide your favorite chopsticks inside, or elevate the basic disposable version with these cases.

Charming Chopstick Cases

You will need:

- Scissors
- Paper (basic printer paper will do)
- Bone folder (optional)
- Glue
- Washi tape

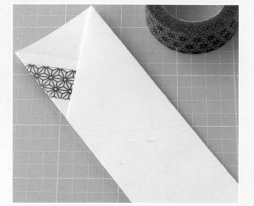

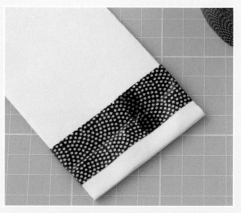

1. Trim the paper to 6½ x 8½ in. (16.5 x 21.5 cm). Follow the folding instructions found on page 125. If desired, use a bone folder to make nice crisp creases. Once the chopstick case is folded, unfold the right half and decorate the top-left angle with a strip of tape. Refold the right half around the case.

2. With the front of the chopstick case facing away from you, glue the back flap in place. Fold the bottom ½ in. (1 cm) of the case up, crease firmly, and secure with tape.

3. Finally, decorate the chopstick case to your liking. Stripes running at the same angle as the case look particularly striking. Whether you add just a few strips or cover the whole case is entirely up to you.

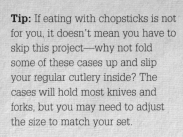

Tip: If eating with chopsticks is not for you, it doesn't mean you have to skip this project—why not fold some of these cases up and slip your regular cutlery inside? The cases will hold most knives and forks, but you may need to adjust the size to match your set.

Fancified Favor Bags

These little bags are perfect for packaging sweet treats and homemade goodies, and your party guests will be thrilled to take home such well-wrapped treats. If you're trying to avoid sugar, use these bags to wrap loot like small toys, and let your guests pick their favorite.

1. Cut the card stock to the desired size—the width of the header card should match the width of the bag, and the length should be double the desired height when folded.

2. Fold the card in half and crease firmly. Now for the fun part—get decorating! Try a different design on each card. Have fun with playful combinations of washi tape stripes and stickers.

3. Fill the clear bags with the desired treats. Place the open end of the bag in the fold of the header card. Staple to secure. For a small bag, one staple in the center should suffice, but for larger bags, two staples are better.

Mess-free Easter Eggs

When Easter rolls around, so many of us long to decorate eggs, but then thoughts turn to fingers stained blue and a heavy scent of vinegar and it all seems like more trouble than it's worth. Washi tape to the rescue—you get all the fun of egg decorating, without any of the mess.

Stripes
Use thin washi tape to create striped patterns on your eggs. To create this look, wrap two strips of tape around the egg vertically, intersecting at the top and bottom. Repeat with a different tape design in the white spaces. Finally, wrap a piece around the middle of the egg if desired.

Collage
Rip or snip small pieces of tape off of the roll and stick to the surface of the egg. Continue layering tape until the desired patchwork look is achieved.

Polka Dots
Apply washi tape to parchment or waxed paper and use a standard hole punch to punch out small circles. Peel the dots off the paper backing and stick randomly to the egg.

Tip: Don't have thin tape? No problem. Apply strips of tape to parchment or waxed paper and cut vertically into thinner strips.

A Christmas Tree for Your Wall

You will need:
- Washi tape
- Craft knife
- Ruler
- Scissors
- Parchment or waxed paper (optional)

Whether you're longing for a tree but just don't have the space, want to add some seasonal spirit throughout the house, or are looking for an idea to corral this year's holiday card haul, creating a washi tape Christmas tree on your wall just might be the solution for you. Creating your washi tape tree each year could become a fun family tradition—it sure is in our house!

Tip: Before committing to any amount of washi tape on your walls, you'll want to test it first in an inconspicuous spot to make sure that it won't damage the paint. While washi tape is compatible with most surfaces, it may peel paint off walls that have many layers of paint or already have some paint chipping off.

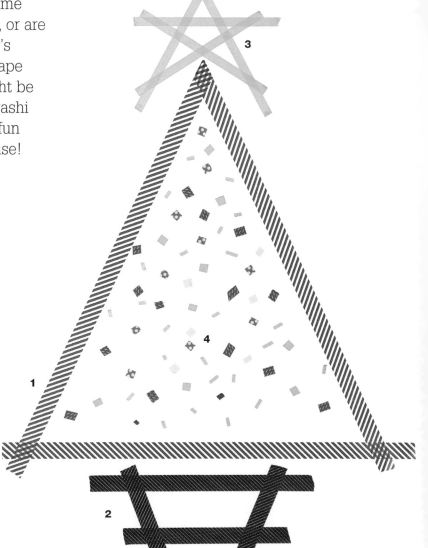

1. Determine the desired height and width of your tree. To create the main part of the tree, you will need to make a large triangle out of tape. Start the tape at the top point of the tree and run the piece at an angle to the desired bottom-left point. Repeat on the right side. Run a third piece of tape across the bottom of the tree, connecting the two sides. Use a craft knife and ruler to carefully trim the points of the tree.

2. Next create your tree stand. Apply a straight piece of washi tape parallel to the bottom of the tree. Apply a second smaller piece under the first. Add a piece on each side, connecting the top and bottom strips and forming a trapezoid. If desired, decorate the tree stand with stripes. Clean up the corners and edges with your craft knife and ruler.

3. Add the topper. Cut five equal lengths of tape. Apply the strips just above the top of your tree, intersecting each one to create a star shape. It helps to imagine drawing a star with tape.

4. Time to decorate your tree! Start by adding small squares of tape to represent the glimmer of Christmas lights. Now add ornaments—you can make your own out of washi tape using the parchment or waxed paper method (see pages 10–11) or tape up lightweight ornaments from your collection, Christmas cards, candy canes, or even create an Advent calendar using small numbered envelopes. Anything goes!

Surprise Heart Pouches

Looking for a unique way to present favors at your next party? Sew up a set of shaped paper pouches. They are the perfect size to hold candy and small trinkets. In this project, washi tape adds not only beauty but also strength.

You will need:
- Marker
- Heart template on page 124 (if desired)
- Kraft paper
- Washi tape
- Scissors
- Sewing machine threaded with thread to match the washi tape

Tip: Hearts are perfect for many occasions, but some celebrations call for different shapes. Try creating surprise pouches in egg shapes for Easter, pumpkins for Halloween, or stockings for Christmas.

1. Using a dark marker, trace the template onto a piece of brown paper. You need to be able to see the marker line through the back of the paper or through the washi tape strips you will be applying in the next step. Check that you can see the line from both sides before step 2.

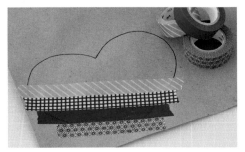

2. Cover the entire shape in strips of washi tape. Make sure to line the strips up next to each other so that there are no gaps and no overlapping sections.

3. Cut the heart shape out of the tape-covered paper. Cut a second heart out of plain paper. Holding the two hearts together, machine sew around the outside edges. Leave a gap of approximately 2 in. (5 cm) in one side.

4. Stuff the heart pouch with the desired treats. Head back to the sewing machine and sew up the gap.

Try hanging a mix of garlands for your next event, or even as a permanent decoration in a kid's room or your craft room. A series of garlands has a greater impact than just one.

Planning your next party? Start with the decorations! Perfect for any occasion, or no occasion at all, these cheerful garlands are quite time consuming but the construction is easy. Simple and sweet flag bunting lets the beauty of washi tape shine, while colorful washi tape shapes sewn together make a bold statement.

Decorative Garlands

Flag bunting

1. Tape a length of twine to your work surface to keep the twine from twisting around while you work. You may need to pull on the ends of the twine from time to time to keep it taut.

2. Cut a length of washi tape approximately 4 in. (10 cm) long. Fold the tape over the twine so that the twine is in the middle of the tape strip. Stick the tape to itself. If you find that the tape is not lining up on the sides, pull it apart again and adjust the alignment. This is easier if you make adjustments before the entire length of the flag is stuck together. Fold the next flag, leaving approximately ¾ in. (2 cm) between the two flags. Continue adding flags, trying to keep spacing consistent as you work.

3. Once your bunting is as long as you'd like, trim the ends of each flag to ensure they are approximately the same length. Finally, cut a notch into the end of each flag. Once finished, string them up and admire your handiwork!

Geometric garlands

1. Cover both sides of a piece of card stock in strips of washi tape. Once the entire sheet is covered, punch or cut out the desired shapes. Circles and triangles are lovely, but you could really pick any shape you desire.

2. Using a sewing machine, sew the shapes together by feeding each shape through the machine one after the other. Leave a little bit of space between each shape to allow for movement. Try to leave the same amount of space between each shape, but don't fret if you don't—with all this color and pattern, your garlands are sure to look fantastic no matter what. You can create a uniform pattern or simply toss all your shapes in a pile and string them together randomly.

Pretty Party Hats

It can be difficult to find the perfect party hat. So, why not make your own? Card stock in pretty colors and a handful of your favorite washi tapes are all you need to make your own fashionable toppers. If you have a creative group of friends, you could even create a hat-decorating station at your next get-together.

You will need:
- Hat template (see page 125)
- Colorful card stock
- Scissors
- Glue
- Thin elastic
- Stapler
- Washi tape

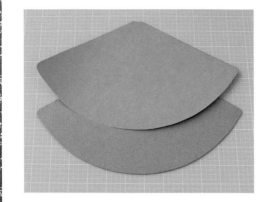

1. Using the template on page 125, trace and cut out the desired number of hats on your chosen card stock.

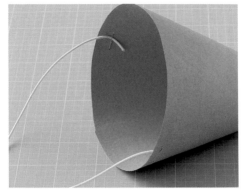

2. Apply glue to one of the edges, then form the hat shape by joining the two straight edges together. Hold securely until the glue sets. Cut a 12-in. (30-cm) length of thin elastic. Test the length of elastic to make sure it fits. Staple one end to each side of the hat.

3. Create a pleated ruffle around the base of the hat. Begin at the back seam and pleat washi tape around the entire base. Try to make your pleats approximately the same size. When you get back around to the start of the ruffle, cut the tape and tuck the loose end under the first pleat.

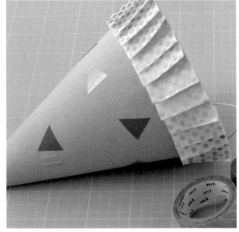

4. Decorate the main part of the hat with small washi tape shapes. A random assortment of small triangles snipped right off the roll or polka dots created using parchment paper look particularly festive.

Tip: Love the idea of making your own hats but don't have the time? Grab a package of plain, store-bought party hats and have fun decorating them.

AROUND THE HOUSE

Washi tape makes a fantastic accent for any home. Dress up simple household items or create your very own art gallery. Craft a unique wall clock or even give furniture a makeover with decorative tape. From the fun to the functional, these projects use tape around the house to beautify objects without breaking the bank.

Quick Starts

Love a satisfyingly quick craft project? Try adding washi tape to basic objects around the house. These simple ideas are wonderful for showcasing your favorite tape designs or for adding a touch of color here and there. The best part? When you get tired of the look, peel off the tape and start again!

Clothespins
Apply washi tape to the flat front and back surfaces of plain wood clothespins. Use a craft knife to trim any excess tape. Pretty pins are perfect for keeping packages closed; alternatively, add a magnet to the back to make a handy fridge clip.

Tea lights
A little bit of washi tape can elevate basic tea lights into something special. Simply wrap a strip of tape around the candle cup. Mix and match different tape designs for a fun arrangement.

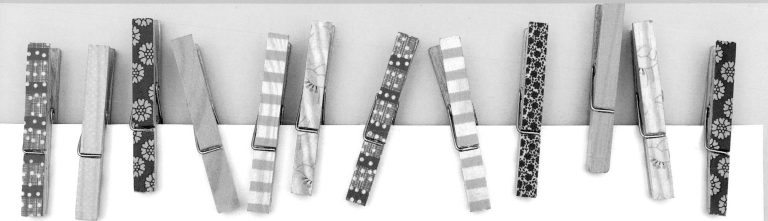

Photo frames

Start with a light-colored frame, then create a layered look with simple strips or go bold and cover the whole frame with tape in contrasting designs. For clean joins, use a craft knife to cut the tape along the frame seams.

Kitchen canisters

Bring some washi style into the kitchen. Dress up plain tins with washi tape dots and stripes, making sure to hide tape ends on the back or in seams. Learn how to create your own washi tape dots on page 11.

Striped Hangers

Basic wooden hangers become their very own fashion statement when you mix and match different colorful patterns. As a bonus, the tape strips add some friction, helping to keep your clothes on the hangers.

Colorblocked Stripes

Create a large block of pattern or color by applying several pieces of tape right in the center of the hanger. Align the tape strips next to each other, matching up the design where possible. Wrap the tape right around the hanger so that both sides are covered. On either side, apply evenly spaced strips in complementary shades. Repeat the arrangement of stripes on the lower hanger bar, taking care to match the positions of the stripes.

Vertical Stripes

Wrap short strips of tape around the hanger to create stripes. Try to keep the stripes evenly spaced. Striped hangers look great no matter what thickness of tape you choose. For the best results, try to avoid applying tape to tricky corners.

Intersecting Stripes

Apply long strips of tape along the flat front surfaces of the hanger, overlapping at the top point and continuing the tape onto the back along the same flat portion. If desired, finish with a small washi tape heart.

To create washi tape hearts, apply tape to parchment or waxed paper before cutting the shape. Then peel and stick!

66

Terrific Twist Ties

With washi tape in your craft cupboard, there's no reason why even the simplest of objects around your home have to be boring. Sandwich basic twist ties between two strips of washi tape and turn them into something far less likely to be lost in the depths of your junk drawer. Pretty twist ties are perfect for use in your kitchen or for wrapping up homemade goodies as a gift.

You will need:
- Washi tape
- White twist ties
- Scissors

Tip: No white twist ties on hand? Use a length of thin wire instead. It's a bit fussy to work with, but is just as effective.

1. Cut a piece of tape approximately 5-in. (12.5-cm) long. Secure to your work surface with the sticky side facing up. Place a twist tie in the center of the tape strip.

2. Cut a 5-in. (12.5-cm) piece of complementary tape. Carefully align it with the first piece and smooth it in place, with the twist tie sandwiched in between. Make sure that the long edges line up and there are no wrinkles. It is much easier to peel apart the tape and fix any alignment issues before the second piece of tape is fully in place.

3. Use scissors to trim the ends of the tie into shape. I love the look of notched ribbon ends, but they are just as lovely with straight or angled ends.

Tip: To make it easier to sandwich your twist tie, stick your initial piece of tape down with slim tape ends. Then it's a simple case of adding the top layer of tape.

Design-a-Clock

Treat yourself to a little wall candy! Create a one-of-a-kind timepiece using your favorite washi tape designs and a wooden clock kit. Colorful numbers mark the hours on the neutral clock face and add some fun to watching the clock. This playful project will be right at home on the wall of your family room or kitchen. For a more sophisticated look, choose monochromatic tape designs or more muted colors.

For a different look, try using washi tape dots in a rainbow of colors to mark each hour.

You will need:

- Mirror printouts of numbers
- Scissors
- Parchment or waxed paper
- Washi tape
- Fine-tipped marker in a dark color
- Craft knife or hole punch
- Wooden clock face
- Clock mechanism and hands

1. Print out the mirror image of numbers 3, 6, 9, and 12. Choose a font size to match the size of your clock face. Cut out each number, leaving a rectangular border around each one.

2. Place the printed numbers face down on the right side of the parchment or waxed paper. Use two short strips of washi tape to secure in place.

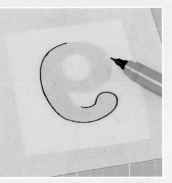

3. Flip the paper over and trace the outline of each number with a fine-tipped marker. Make sure that you can see the lines through the paper.

4. Flip the paper back over and remove the number printout. Starting from one side, apply strips of tape in consecutive order, making sure that each strip slightly overlaps the one before. If using patterned tape, try to match the pattern where possible.

5. Once the numbers are covered with tape, flip the paper back over and use the number outlines as cutting guides. To cut out enclosed sections, start by punching a hole or use a craft knife.

6. Place the numbers at the corresponding 3, 6, 9, and 12 o'clock positions on the wooden clock face. Once you're happy with the placement, carefully peel each number off the paper, starting at the bottommost strip, and stick to the clock face.

7. Assemble your clock using the instructions included with the clock mechanism. If desired, cover the clock hands with washi tape. Cut around the edges of the hands using a craft knife.

Washi Tape Gallery Wall

Build a beautiful art wall or photo gallery without a pricey trip to the frame shop. Washi tape frames are a fun way to add some color and interest to a blank wall. Size your frames for specific prints and photos, or create the frames and switch out the art to suit the season (or your mood). Combine different frame styles and sizes for a more interesting gallery.

Tip: Please refer to the information on page 13 before sticking washi tape on your walls.

1. Tape a piece of paper to the wall of the same size as your desired photo or art print. Leaving a space of approximately ½ in. (1 cm) between the paper and the tape, create a border around the paper with four strips of washi tape. The strips should overlap at the corners.

2. Create a second tape box around the first, leaving approximately 3 in. (7.5 cm) between the two lines of tape. Make sure that the strips overlap at the corners.

3. Using your craft knife and ruler, trim the four corners of each tape box. Use a light touch, making sure you only cut through the tape and not into the wall. Next, place your ruler at an angle and create mitered joins at each of the corners.

4. Apply short strips of tape from the inside corners of the outer frame to the outside corners of the inner frame. Clean up the ends with your craft knife and ruler.

You will need:
- Paper
- Washi tape
- Craft knife
- Ruler

5. Repeat with the next frame. Continue adding frames of various shapes and styles until the desired look is achieved. Tape art and photos or hang small objects in the empty frames.

Mix frames of different styles and colors then fill with your favorite images to create a unique art gallery. Switch out the art on display as new work finds its way into your home.

Vases

Sure, flowers are beautiful—but why should they have all the fun? Add some color to plain glass or ceramic vases with a little washi tape. Your vase will continue to be worthy of display even after the blooms inside have faded away.

Tip: Choose straight-sided round or square vases for this project. It is difficult to apply tape to fluted or scalloped surfaces.

Vertical Stripes
Keep your vertical stripes evenly spaced by placing the first four stripes at 12 o'clock, 3 o'clock, 6 o'clock, and 9 o'clock. Then fill in the spaces between with more stripes.

Horizontal Stripes
Apply evenly spaced horizontal stripes of tape around the vase. You can apply stripes all the way up the height of the vase or try a grouping of three stripes for a simpler look.

Creative Designs
Don't stop there—you can dress your vase to suit any occasion. Need more ideas? Try a sprinkling of confetti triangles, add polka dots, or create layers of tape for a ribbon effect.

Custom Coasters

Pretty washi tape stripes transform basic wooden coasters into mini works of art. Display your favorite tape designs or make different sets to match your seasonal dishes. You could even wrap up a set of these coasters for a lovely handmade housewarming gift.

1. Apply stripes of washi tape to the top face of the coasters. Try alternating stripes that run straight up and down, on an angle, or even in a chevron design.

2. Using scissors, trim the tape ends so that they are flush with the edges of the coaster. If you would prefer, place the coaster face down on a cutting mat and trim the tape ends using a craft knife.

3. Coat the top and sides of the coasters with two coats of découpage glue. Allow to dry thoroughly between coats. Most découpage glues include a sealant that is water resistant—if you're worried about water damage, you can apply a finishing layer of acrylic sealant.

To create chevron stripes, apply angled strips that intersect in the middle of the coaster. Using a craft knife and a ruler, cut a straight line down the center of the coaster where the strips intersect and carefully remove the extra tape ends.

Name Garland

Not just for names, this garland is a great way to celebrate pretty much any occasion. Create a LOVE garland for Valentine's Day or the happy couple's initials for an engagement party.

Hang this personalized garland on a bedroom door or above a crib to welcome a special child to their very own room. Make one as a gift or use as a party decoration. The garland is lovely in stripes of different washi tape colors and patterns.

You will need:
- Scissors
- Card stock—standard 8½ x 11 in. (21.5 x 28 cm)
- Washi tape
- Small hole punch
- Twine, string, or ribbon

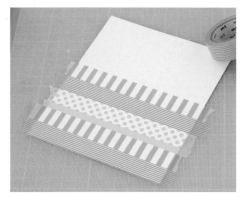

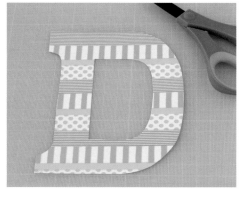

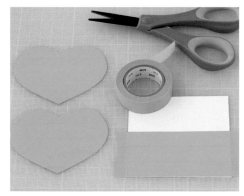

1. Each piece of card stock will make four letters. Start by cutting the card stock into four equal pieces of 4¼ x 5½ in. (10.75 x 14 cm). Cover each piece of card stock with strips of washi tape. Ensure you line the strips up next to each other without leaving any blank space or overlapping tape.

2. Cut each letter out of the washi-covered card. You can cut freehand or sketch the desired letter backward onto the back of the card before cutting. To cut out enclosed areas, first punch a hole to make cutting easier or use a craft knife. For names that contain multiples of the same letter, use your first letter as a template for cutting the others.

3. Once all letters are cut out, it's time to add some embellishment to the garland. Cut two pieces of 3 x 3½ in. (7.5 x 9 cm) card. Choose one color or design of tape that coordinates with your letters. Cover the squares in tape. Cut out hearts or other desired shapes.

4. Use a small hole punch to create holes in the tops of the letters and hearts. For each upper portion of a letter, you will want to punch two holes. Thread the twine or ribbon through the holes to create your garland.

Decorate Your Furniture

Boring furniture got you down? Add some washi flavor to spruce it up! Colorful stripes and blocks of pattern will add some cheer to your home. Using tape instead of paint ensures that you can change the look on a whim without the mess (or the fumes) that usually accompany furniture makeovers. Let's start with the humble chair.

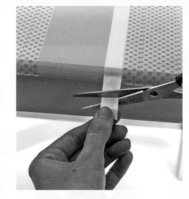

1. Determine whether you'd like to cover the entire chair with tape or only selected portions. Since this project will use quite a bit of tape, it's a good idea to plan out which tape goes where before you start. Making a quick sketch can help.

2. Working on each part of the chair individually, begin applying strips of tape to the chair. Tape strips should be aligned so that there are no gaps or overlapping sections.

3. Continue adding tape until all desired surfaces are covered in tape. Use your scissors or craft knife to trim rough tape edges.

4. Washi tape is perfect for temporary makeovers, but if you want to make it more permanent, you need to cover the washi tape with a sealant for durability. Apply several layers of acrylic sealant, allowing it to dry thoroughly between coats.

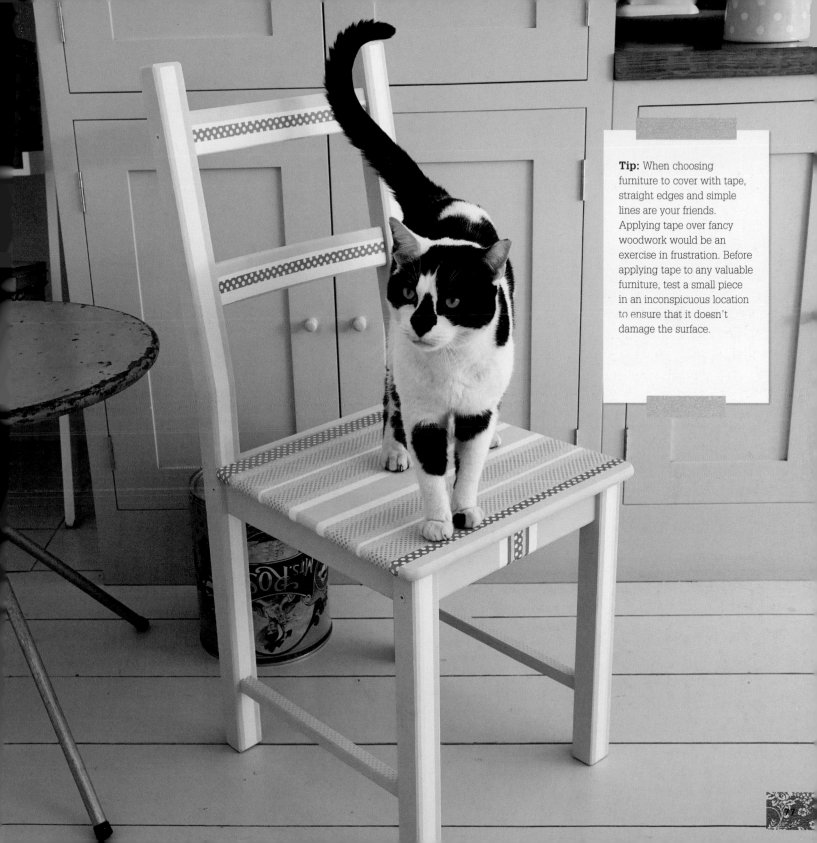

Tip: When choosing furniture to cover with tape, straight edges and simple lines are your friends. Applying tape over fancy woodwork would be an exercise in frustration. Before applying tape to any valuable furniture, test a small piece in an inconspicuous location to ensure that it doesn't damage the surface.

Simple shapes look striking in a stack.

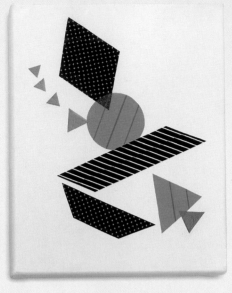

Try your hand at a little abstract art.

Intersecting lines are bold, but simple.

Canvas Art

Sometimes you're in the mood to create something a little more arty and a little less crafty. Creating your own art using washi tape can be a great opportunity to let your inner artist out to play. Affordable pre-stretched canvases available from your local art or craft store are a wonderful surface to create on—they provide a more professional finished piece and, should you wish to "paint" something new, the tape peels off easily so you can start afresh.

Tip: When creating your own washi tape artwork, you can work from a sketch or make it up as you go along. The washi tape makes it easy to remove components that aren't working; however, be careful when you remove and re-stick the tape numerous times, as you may create creases in the tape.

You will need:
- Scissors
- Washi tape
- Parchment or waxed paper
- Pre-stretched and primed canvas

1. Apply overlapping strips of washi tape to a piece of parchment or waxed paper. Cut out the desired shapes. If desired, draw the required shapes on the back of the paper before cutting.

2. Arrange the shapes on the canvas. Take the time to determine where each piece will go before removing the backing.

3. Once you are happy with your arrangement, peel the paper backing off each shape and position it on the canvas. If needed, carefully peel the shapes off the canvas and reposition.

4. As a finishing touch, apply a strip of tape around the outside edge of the canvas. This optional step creates a frame for your art.

Decorative Letters

Add something custom to your bookshelf, gallery wall, or mantel with a fun, decorative letter. Spell out a sweet message or craft up a letter for each member of the family. No matter how many you make, or where you display them, you'll love creating these one-of-a-kind monograms.

1. Cover the front of the letter with strips of washi tape. You can mix and match different patterns or stick with just one. If using just one design, be sure to line up the pattern, if possible.

2. Use a craft knife to clean up the edges, cutting off the washi tape ends.

3. Wrap tape around the outer and inner surfaces of the letter. Align the tape strips next to each other without overlapping. Try to place the tape ends on the bottom of the letter where they will be hidden.

Ever-blooming Flowers

Washi tape flowers are a wonderful source of color for your home, whatever the season. A little bit tricky at first, once you get the hang of flower making, you won't want to stop. Washi tape flowers also make lovely gift toppers or you could use them to decorate each place setting at your next dinner party—they make a delightful memento for your guests to take home.

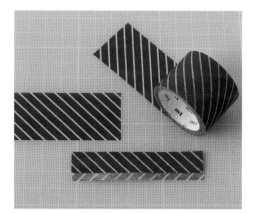

1. Choose a 1¼-in. (30-mm) tape for the center of your flower. Cut a piece approximately 3 in. (7.5 cm) long. Fold the tape along the length, sticking the two sides together and leaving approximately ¼ in. (6 mm) of tape uncovered at the bottom.

You will need:

- Washi tape: 1¼ in. (30 mm) wide for petals and stamens; ⅝ in. (15 mm) wide for leaves and stem
- Scissors
- Floral wire

4. Build the flower by adding each petal to the wire. Work in a circular motion, creating layers of petals, each slightly lower on the wire than the one before. Secure by wrapping the sticky ends of the petals around the wire. Use your fingers to shape each petal as you go.

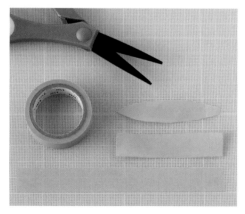

5. To make the leaves, cut three pieces of ⅝-in. (15 mm) washi tape, each approximately 5 in. (12.5 cm) long. Fold the tape, aligning the side edges, and sticking it to itself. Leave ⅜ in. (1 cm) uncovered at one end. Cut into leaf shapes.

2. Cut the folded part of the tape into a fringe, taking care not to cut all the way through. Wrap the fringed tape around one end of a piece of floral wire, with the sticky part of the tape facing inward to secure.

3. Choose a 1¼-in. (30-mm) tape for the petals of your flower. For each petal, cut a piece of tape approximately 3 in. (7.5 cm) long. Fold the tape along the width, sticking the top down and leaving approximately ⅜ in. (1 cm) uncovered. Cut into a rounded petal shape. You will need 10 to 12 petals for each flower.

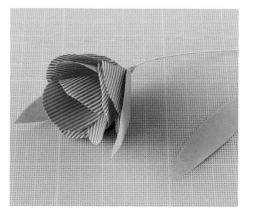

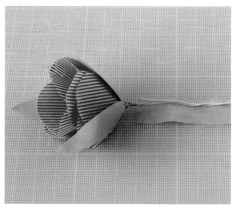

6. Evenly space leaves around the outside of the flower. Secure them in place by wrapping the sticky ends around the wire slightly below the bottom of the flower.

7. If desired, you can fold thin and long wires in half and loosely twist them together to create sturdier stems. Wrap the entire wire in washi tape. Cut one long strip of tape the same length as the stem, lay the wire onto the tape, and wrap around. To finish, wrap a short piece of tape around the area where the leaves and stem meet.

GET ORGANIZED

Being organized and getting some work done doesn't have to be boring, especially with washi tape in your corner. Customize basic office supplies, decorate pencils and notebooks, create custom bookmarks, or even learn how to turn your tape into labels. You'll love adding your creative style to items that you use every day.

We spend so many hours in our offices, shouldn't we have a little fun while we're at it? Adding some washi tape to basic office supplies is a great way to inject a little color and personality into your daily life.

Quick Starts

Paperclip Bookmarks

Transform simple paperclips into clever bookmarks and document flags with a few strips of washi tape. To keep things from getting too fiddly, start with jumbo paperclips. Cut a piece of washi tape approximately 4 in. (10 cm) long. Slide it sideways into the center of the clip, then turn so that the top edge of the clip is positioned in the center of the strip. Stick the two sides of the tape together and trim ends into the desired shape. For less bulk, cut notches in the center of the tape strip before applying it to the clip.

Binder Clips

Add a little washi style to even the bulkiest of documents with these colorful binder clips. Apply strips of tape to each side of the clip. Stay monochromatic or add more fun by using a different color and pattern on each side.

Pushpins

Basic tacks get a quick makeover with a little help from washi tape. Cut a small strip of tape and stick the tack top down right in the center of it. Cut the tape into a circle around the tack head, then snip notches all the way around the tape circle. Fold the edges of the tape toward the underside of the tack. Smooth out any wrinkles on the surface. For added durability, apply a layer of découpage glue.

Need a home for all those pretty pushpins? Learn how to customize a bulletin board with tape on page 92.

Pretty Pencils

Standard pencils don't have to be boring—a few minutes and a few feet of your favorite washi tape are all that separate you from writing in style. Looking for a great back-to-school gift idea? Why not craft up a set of pretty pencils for your kids or your favorite teacher?

Tip: Most washi tapes are quite translucent. For best results, choose pencils that are neutral in color, such as traditional pencil yellow, natural wood, or white.

1. Starting at the eraser end of the pencil, apply the washi tape at an angle. The end of the tape should overlap the metal ring by about ½ in. (1.5 cm).

2. Holding the tape taut in one hand, turn the pencil with the other, wrapping the tape around as you go. Ensure that the tape lies flat on the pencil without any wrinkles or bubbles. Each round of tape should slightly overlap the one before it. If there are gaps or tape overlaps too much, unwind and try a different angle. Continue wrapping until pencil is fully covered. Use a craft knife to trim excess tape from the metal ring.

3. Apply a thin layer of découpage glue over the taped surface of the pencil. Allow the pencil to dry thoroughly before sharpening.

For more fun, wrap your pencil with two slim tape designs or add a layer of extra-skinny tape.

Striped version Starting at the eraser end, apply a horizontal stripe of tape to the pencil. Make sure to slightly overlap the tape ends. Continue to add stripes of different colored tapes until the pencil is fully covered.

Noteworthy Notebooks

Pocket-sized notebooks are perfect for keeping track of to-do lists, sketching interesting passersby, and jotting down dreams. With washi tape, you can design your ideal notebook so that the outside is just as interesting as what's inside.

Start with a blank covered notebook in a light or neutral color. Pick your favorite palette of washi tape colors and designs. Have fun applying stripes of tape in the desired pattern. You can completely cover the outside of the notebook or simply add a few strips. Trim the tape ends at the edges.

If you handle your notebook a great deal or it spends a lot of time in the bottom of your purse, you may want to apply a coat of découpage glue for added durability.

Tip: There are plenty of notebooks with black covers out there. Walk away. Nobody wins when you try to decorate a black notebook; true washi tape is too translucent to play nicely with such a dark color.

Make your own pattern with strips and stripes of different widths and designs. Or why not add a tape monogram? Turn to page 36 for instructions.

Bookmarks

Bookmarks are a wonderful small-scale canvas for playing with washi tape. Practice different techniques and try out various tape combinations while crafting usable objects. Before you know it, you'll have a lovely handmade bookmark tucked inside all your favorite books and not a dog-eared corner in sight!

You will need:
- Card stock
- Washi tape
- Ruler
- Scissors
- Hole punch (optional)
- Baker's twine or colorful string (optional)

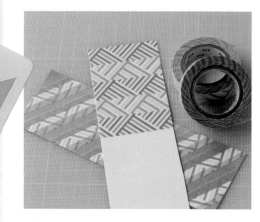

1. Start with a 2 x 6-in. (5 x 15-cm) piece of light-colored card stock. Apply strips of washi tape to both sides of the bookmark. Try horizontal stripes or wrap the tape around diagonally. Leave lots of blank space or cover the entire surface with tape. It's up to you.

5. Cut a second 12-in. (30-cm) length of twine. Position one end so that it lines up with the bottom of the tassel loop, then wrap the other end around the top of the loop approximately 10 times to create the tassel shape. Tuck the loose end under the wrapped twine, running the remaining piece of twine down into the tassel.

2. For a softer look, you can round the corners of the bookmark with your scissors or a corner rounder. If adding a tassel, punch a small hole in the center top edge of the bookmark.

3. To make a tassel, first cut a piece of twine approximately 12 in. (30 cm) long. Set aside—this will be your tie string. Wrap twine around four of your fingers approximately 20 times. Cut the end.

4. Place the tie string inside the loop of twine on your fingers and position at the top. Carefully slide the tassel loop off of your fingers. Knot the tie string once around the top of the tassel loop.

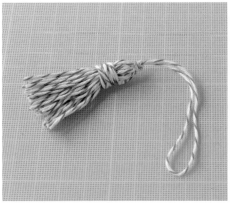

8. Loop the string through the hole to attach the tassel to your bookmark. Time to read and enjoy!

6. Cut open the bottom of the tassel loop. Trim the tassel to the desired length, ensuring that the ends are even.

7. Untie the tie string at the top of the tassel, but do not remove. Tie the free ends together, then trim the ends. Turn the tie string so that the knot is inside the top loop of the tassel. Tie a second knot on top of the tassel.

Learn the trick to creating stickers from specialty tapes on page 11.

Customized Washi Tape

1. Start by printing out the desired text on a standard inkjet printer. Play with different text sizes and fonts until you find the right look for your particular project.

Use washi tape to affix pictures and other ephemera into scrapbooks—it's cute and easy! Most washi tape is acid free and archival quality, but not all tapes are made equal. It's always a good idea to check first.

Though it is possible to find washi tape with words and phrases, it doesn't always say what you want. With this clever trick, you can say pretty much anything with washi tape. Use it to add highlighted text to your schedule or scrapbook, for labeling jars in the pantry, or even as a special touch when wrapping gifts.

2. Cut a piece of washi tape a little bit longer than the printed text. Try to choose tape with light colors or subtle patterns to allow the text to be more prominent.

3. Lay the strip of tape over the printed text. Gently run your finger over the text area a couple of times to help the ink transfer to the tape.

4. Carefully peel the tape off of the printout and apply wherever you please. The tape will curl as you remove it, especially when working with longer strips, so use both hands.

Glass jars

Glass jars look particularly charming when holding your paintbrushes or other tools in your craft or art studio. Thoroughly wash and dry empty jars. For easier label removal, try soaking the jar in hot water before peeling the label off. When your jar is clean and dry, apply washi tape to the flat surfaces. Evenly spaced stripes look fresh or try layering different widths for more interest. Not a fan of stripes? Add confetti triangles using a variety of different tapes.

Cardboard containers

Cardboard containers, like the ones that usually hold chocolate powder, make great vessels for pens, pencils, and the other bits and pieces in your junk drawer. Once you peel off the paper label, there's generally a blank cardboard surface with straight sides, perfect for adding a little washi love. Cover the entire surface with strips of washi tape. Fill with all those errant writing utensils and never again wonder where all your pens have gone!

Glass jars with a little washi love can also double as casual vases. Why not pick a posy of your favorite flowers from the garden and place in a washi-taped jar on your kitchen windowsill? It's a lovely pick-me-up to gaze at while doing the washing up.

Upcycled Containers

Need a little more storage in your home office or craft studio? Don't we all! One of the nice things about washi tape is that it so easily transforms ordinary objects into something a little more special. Next time you're about to toss an empty container into the recycling bin, ask yourself, can I washi that? Chances are, the answer is yes!

Woven Washi Clipboard

Have you ever tried weaving with washi tape? The classic over/under pattern of basket weaving looks quite lovely when created out of translucent washi tape, as different colors appear when you layer two shades of tape. The smooth surface of a clipboard is also an ideal surface for practicing this technique as the tape quite easily peels off, which is useful as you'll be moving it around quite a bit.

You will need:
- Clipboard
- Washi tape
- Craft knife
- Scissors

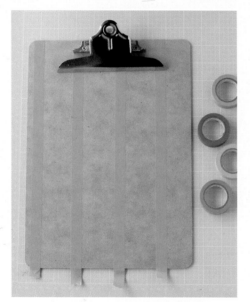

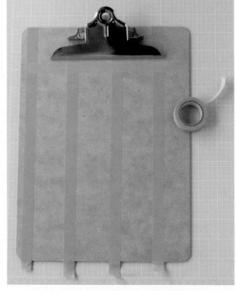

1. Choose your desired washi tapes. I think an even number of colors looks best. Apply four vertical strips of tape from the top to the bottom of the clipboard. Ensure that the strips are evenly spaced across the width of the board. At the top edge, wrap the tape ends around to the back or trim at the edge of the clip using a craft knife.

2. Run your first horizontal strip of washi along the top of the clipboard, slightly below the clip. Wrap the tape ends around the edges.

3. Apply four more strips of tape lengthwise, centering them in the spaces in between the original four strips.

Love the idea of transforming basic clipboards into something special, but not sold on all this weaving business? Dress them up in whatever washi way you please! They're particularly cute decorated with some washi tape pencils.

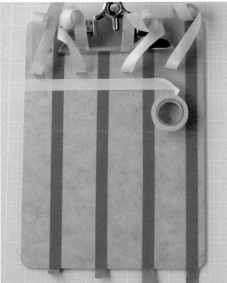

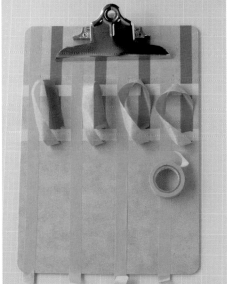

4. Next, peel back the original four vertical strips of tape to the first horizontal strip. Once they are out of the way, apply the second horizontal strip across the width of the clipboard, wrapping the ends around to the back. Replace the loose vertical tape strips so that they overlap the horizontal strip you just applied. You can now see the woven pattern taking shape.

5. Continue applying tape strips along the width of the clipboard, using the over/under weaving technique. Once the surface of the clipboard is fully decorated, wrap the free bottom ends of the lengthwise strips around to the back of the board. If you find that tape ends have lost their stickiness due to all the repositioning, use a little découpage glue to secure them in place.

Bulletin Board

A standard wood frame corkboard is useful, but usually not that pretty. Give your basic bulletin board a glamorous washi tape makeover with just a handful of tapes and a few free minutes. The benefit of choosing washi tape over another material for this project is that you can change up the look of your board to match your mood, the season, or the color scheme of your latest project with very little effort.

Tip: Use a variety of different tape designs or stick with your favorite one.

Tip: If desired, make colorful tacks to match your board. For tips, turn to page 83.

1. Choose a selection of coordinating tapes. I think this project looks best with two or three.

2. Start by applying tape to the front facing edges of the frame. Lay a strip along the top edge, ensuring that the tape runs straight across. Trim the tape edges by cutting along the mitered join of each of the frame's corners with a craft knife. Repeat these steps with the remaining 3 edges.

3. Starting with a bottom corner, apply washi tape in one long strip all along the outside edge of the frame. Smooth tape as you apply, ensuring any extra tape width is folded around to the back of the frame. Pay special attention to corners.

4. Hang your beautiful new board and fill with inspiration pictures and important notes.

Tip: For even more fun, use spray glue and pretty paper to cover the cork surface of your board.

Make Magnets

To create your own washi tape magnets, you will need printable magnet sheets from your local office supply store. This product features a blank white front and a magnetized back. The white front is ideal for use with washi tape.

Though these magnets aren't super strong (they will hold a piece of paper or a photo but not a whole stack of them) they will add some fun and function to whatever magnetized surface you please.

Want to simply add a little washi tape flavor to your fridge? Apply a strip of washi tape across the width of the magnet paper, aligning with the top edge. Cut along the bottom edge of the washi strip. You will now have one long washi tape magnet. Cut into the desired magnet lengths. If you wish, you can create a more authentic-looking washi tape strip magnet by trimming the edges into a torn or serrated look.

One of the nicest things about the magnet sheets is that they are thin enough to cut into shapes using a punch. Cover a magnet sheet with washi tape in a variety of colors and patterns. Use your favorite punches to create custom shaped magnets.

Feeling extra fancy? Why not create food-themed magnets! Ice-cream cones with colorful scoops and a cherry on top are a cute way to add some personality to your kitchen—and to hold this week's menu plan. Sketch the desired shape onto the magnet sheet, then apply strips of tape, making sure to align any patterns if possible. Cut out the shapes. Use a fine permanent marker to draw on any extra details.

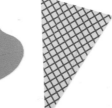

Keep-It-Together Envelope Book

This clever envelope book might just be the simplest bookbinding project you'll ever try, but it definitely doesn't look like it. By using tape to connect each of the envelope pages, there's a nice balance of form and function on each page. Use the envelopes to organize stickers and other small craft supplies or to keep track of important receipts and business cards. Or why not pack one on your next vacation? You can use each envelope to collect small pieces of paper ephemera from your travels.

You will need:

- Thin chipboard or card stock
- 5 to 10 envelopes
- Washi tape
- Scissors

As you fill your envelopes with bits and pieces, your book will grow bigger and bigger. If desired, create a bellyband out of elastic or tie a length of colorful string around the book to keep everything in place.

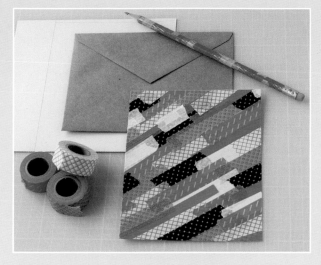

1. First, create the front and back covers of the book. Using one of the envelopes as a template, cut two pieces of chipboard or card stock to the same size. Decorate one side of each cover with washi tape.

2. Start building your book by connecting two envelopes together with a strip of washi tape. The page on the left side should be the back of the envelope, the page on the right side should be the front. Continue to tape envelopes together until all the pages are connected. Trim any tape ends.

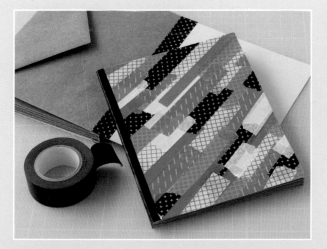

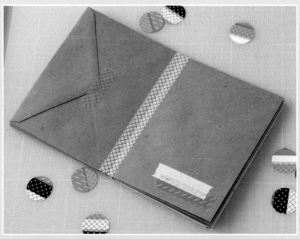

3. Use the same technique to add the front and back covers of your book. Finally, using a strip of wide washi tape, cover the spine of the book, wrapping the edges of the tape around to the front and back covers.

4. Use the front of the envelopes to write notes or to label the contents. The envelopes can be used to hold whatever small and light things you please. Add a small strip of tape to each envelope flap to help keep the contents inside.

ACCESSORIES

Wear your washi in style! With the help of some simple techniques and materials, you can transform washi tape into wearable art. Ranging from bold to whimsical, these accessory projects include earrings, bangles, brooches, and beads. You'll be amazed at the modern on-trend jewelry and accessories that you can create using tape.

Quick Starts

Washi tape-covered boxes are a wonderful option for storing your jewelry collection. Or why not make one to match a washi tape gift for a loved one? These cute reusable boxes are the perfect way to present your handmade accessories.

Heart-shaped box

For a simple yet bold look, cover your box in blocks of color. When applying each strip of tape, do your best to match the pattern. For curvy shapes like this heart, snip loose tape edges every ⅛ in. (3 mm) or so before folding it onto the bottom or around the lip of the lid.

Monogrammed box

Cover the bottom half of the box with diagonal stripes in your favorite combination of solids and patterns. Top with a letter made of tape. For details on how to make a monogram out of tape, turn to page 36.

Dots and stripes

Horizontal stripes and polka dots combine for a playful look. When covering the bottom half of the box, start at the top edge and work your way down. Fold the extra tape around to the bottom of the box.

Tip: Papier mâché boxes from your local craft store are a wonderful option for customizing with tape. Or why not give new life to the boring small boxes often received with jewelry purchases?

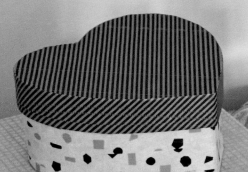

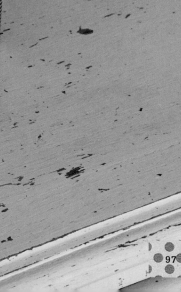

Colorblocked studs More color, more fun! Create colorblocked stud earrings by combining two washi tape designs on each wood shape. Make sure to line up the tapes so that the edges meet without overlapping or leaving any gaps.

Mix and match Don't feel the need to follow the crowd with matching studs. Why not mix up your color and shape choices for each pair?

Gold line Add some interest to solid color studs with a slash of color. Once the main color is applied, add a thin strip of washi tape in a metallic or contrasting color.

Stud Earrings

Design your perfect stud earrings using washi tape and lightweight wooden shapes. Craft an assortment of different colors and shapes, then mix and match to suit your mood (and your outfit). Lightweight wood veneer shapes from the scrapbooking section of your local craft store are perfect for this project. Make sure to choose ones with simple lines to avoid headaches when cutting around the edges.

You will need:
- Wood veneer shapes, approx. ⅜ in–½ in. (10–12 mm)
- Washi tape
- Scissors
- Decoupage glue
- Paintbrush
- Earring posts and backs
- Jewelry glue

1. Stick washi tape to the front surface of your wood shapes. Carefully cut the tape to size by guiding your scissors around the edges of the shape. Try to cut in one smooth motion to prevent jagged edges.

2. Apply a coat of découpage glue to the front and sides of the washi-covered wood shapes with a paintbrush to keep the tape in place. Allow to dry thoroughly. If desired, you can add a second coat of glue.

3. Once the shape is fully dry, flip it over and glue the earring post to the back. For durability, use a strong glue designed for jewelry making. Allow to dry thoroughly (for up to 24 hours) before wearing.

1. Start with a light wood bangle and washi tapes in your desired colors and patterns. Decide whether you'd like your stripes to run on an angle or straight up and down. Straight-sided bangles look great either way while bangles with a more rounded shape are better suited to angled stripes.

2. Apply the first stripe, wrapping the edges around to the inside of the bangle. Smooth out any wrinkles. Add the second stripe, following the edges of the first. On straight-sided bangles, you will be able to align the strips without overlapping. On rounded-sided bangles, the strips will overlap slightly at the top and bottom. Continue adding strips of tape until the entire surface of your bangle is covered.

3. Finish by applying a coat of découpage glue to the entire surface of your bangle, inside and out. If you would prefer to be able to easily reinvent your bangle to match different outfits, you may want to skip this step. An uncoated bracelet looks just as smashing; however, you may find that the surface gets dirty quickly and the tape ends might unstick after a few outings.

Tip: Want to washi but not so keen on the striped look? You can definitely wrap a single washi design around a bangle; however, choose a busier pattern like a multicolor floral. The overlapping edges and mismatched patterns of a wrapped bracelet can look a bit messy with a simple washi pattern.

Bangle Bracelets

You might be iffy about wearing your heart on your sleeve, but you'll definitely want to wear washi on your wrist! An armload of bold bangles adds personality to even the most basic of little black dresses. Whether you wear one or a whole stack, your custom bracelet is sure to be a statement piece.

Bold Brooches

Brooches are a fashionable way to show off your washi style. Make your own by dressing up simple wooden shapes with washi tape. Wear one big bold brooch or make a variety of smaller ones and pin on a trio of different designs.

You will need:
- Wooden shapes, approx. 1½–3 in. (4–7.5 cm)
- Washi tape
- Scissors
- Découpage glue
- Paintbrush
- Pin back
- Jewelry glue

One washi design is fun, but multiple patterns on one brooch look fantastic. Apply strips of washi tape in a variety of your favorite colors and patterns. You can overlap strips or simply align them side by side.

1. Cover the front of the desired wooden shape in pieces of washi tape. Make sure you align edges and patterns without overlapping edges.

2. Carefully cut around the edges of the shape with a pair of scissors, removing the excess tape as you go. Try to follow the edge of the shape with your scissors and cut in a smooth motion to avoid jagged edges.

3. Apply a coat of découpage glue to the front and sides of the washi-covered wooden shape with a paintbrush to keep the tape in place. Allow to dry thoroughly.

4. When the shape is fully dry, flip it over and glue the pin back to the center using jewelry glue. Allow to dry thoroughly (for up to 24 hours) before wearing.

Modern Beads

Plain wooden beads and pendants are instantly elevated with a little washi tape love. These easy projects are a play on the trend of painted wooden or ceramic beads strung together into chunky necklaces.

Washi pendants

Create a mini masterpiece using just tape and a flat wooden pendant. Apply intersecting strips of tape or create blocks of color. Use a craft knife to carefully shape and trim tape on the surface of the pendant without damaging the surface. Trim around the edges of the pendant with scissors and make sure to punch through the hole with a pen or your craft knife. Finish with 1–2 coats of découpage glue before stringing onto a chain or a colorful piece of cord.

Tip: While coating your beads in découpage glue, try holding each bead on a toothpick. This way you'll avoid touching the bead and ruining the surface.

Confetti beads

Tiny confetti-like triangles of tape are a modern version of polka dots. Cut a small piece of tape from the roll and then snip it into small triangle shapes. Apply randomly to the surface of an unfinished wooden bead. Stick with one color of tape or have fun with multiple shades. Apply 1–2 coats of découpage glue to seal your creation. Allow to dry thoroughly (for up to 24 hours) before wearing.

Geometric beads

Faceted geometric wooden beads are well loved by contemporary jewelry makers. Get the look of paint without the mess by covering individual sides of the beads in pretty colors of tape. Here's how: Apply a small piece of tape to one side. Place face down on a cutting mat and cut around the edges with a craft knife. Repeat with each flat side. When you're satisfied with your creation, apply 1–2 coats of découpage glue. Allow to dry thoroughly (for up to 24 hours) before wearing.

Washi Jewel Rings

Transform your favorite tape designs into wearable jewels. Convenient epoxy dome stickers have the look of resin without the tedium of waiting for it to set (or the toxic smell). With this simple project, you can whip up a whole wardrobe of lustworthy rings in a single sitting. A great "crafternoon" project to do with friends!

Tip: Epoxy stickers and jewelry settings are available in a multitude of shapes and sizes. Why not try making other accessories such as pendant necklaces or cabochon bracelets with this technique?

1. Apply washi tape to the flat setting. Use a single tape design or combine two or more different patterns. Ensure the tape covers the entire surface of the setting.

2. Turn the ring over so that the setting is flat on your cutting mat and use a craft knife to trim the excess tape from around the setting. Carefully peel away the extra tape.

3. Press an epoxy dome sticker into the ring setting over the tape. Be careful not to get any fingerprints or dust on the sticky side of the sticker.

You will need:
- Ring blanks with flat setting, approx. ⅜ in. (10 mm)
- Washi tape
- Scissors
- Craft knife
- Epoxy dome stickers in matching size, approx. ⅜ in. (10 mm)

Vinyl Coin Purse

These cute vinyl pouches are just the right size to hold coins, bus tickets, bobby pins, and other little whatnots. Start with stripes and expand into any design you can dream up. And while you're busy creating tape masterpieces, the vinyl will be working hard to both protect and showcase your washi tape designs.

You will need:

- Clear vinyl
- Ruler or tape measure
- Scissors
- Washi tape
- Sewing machine and thread
- Snap fasteners
- Snap fastener tool
- Hammer

1. Cut two pieces of vinyl approximately 4 in. (10 cm) wide by 8 in. (20 cm) long. Cover one piece of vinyl in strips of washi tape. Five to six strips of standard ⅝ in. (15 mm) width tape make for the perfect pocket-sized pouch. Trim both vinyl pieces to the size of the tape-covered piece.

2. Hold the two pieces of vinyl together so that the tape is sandwiched in between them. Sew along the bottom short edge. Insert the bottom snap approximately 1 in. (2.5 cm) down from the edge.

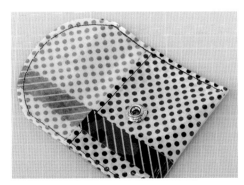

3. Cut the unsewn short end into a rounded shape. Fold the bottom edge up approximately 2½ in. (6.5 cm). Starting at one bottom corner, sew around the outside edge of the pouch, ending at the opposite corner. Trim any excess vinyl edges.

4. Fold the top flap of the pouch down and push against the bottom snap to mark the desired position of the top snap. Insert the top snap in the marked spot.

Hair Candy

You will need:
- Wooden shapes, approx. ¾–1 in. (2–2.5 cm)
- Washi tape
- Scissors
- Découpage glue
- Paintbrush
- Bobby pins with glue pads
- Jewelry glue

There's no such thing as a bad hair day when you've got lovely hair clips to adorn your locks. Cute and colorful shapes on classic bobby pins are a wonderful way to wear washi tape. When you are selecting wooden shapes for this project, stick to simple outlines to avoid frustration.

1. Apply washi tape to the front of your wooden shapes. You can stick with one design only or try mixing and matching different patterns. Carefully cut the excess tape from around the edges, allowing the edge of the wooden shape to guide your scissors.

2. Wrap a piece of washi tape around the outside edge of the wooden shape. For cleaner finishing, snip the overhanging tape every ⅛ in. (3 mm). Fold onto the back of the shape.

Adding tape to the sides of the shape can be a bit tricky. Feel free to skip it if you find it too fiddly. The hair clips are just as cute without!

3. Apply a coat of découpage glue to the front and sides of your shape with a paintbrush. When it is thoroughly dry, flip it over and apply a coat to the back, ensuring that the tape edges stay stuck down.

4. Once the découpage glue is dry, it's time to glue your shape to the bobby pin. Apply a small amount of jewelry glue to the glue pad on the bobby pin and then stick it in place on the center back of your wooden shape. Allow to dry thoroughly (for up to 24 hours) before wearing.

Feather Earrings

You will need:

- Wide washi tape, 1¼ in. (30 mm)
- Scissors
- Thin wire
- Standard washi tape, ⅝ in. (15 mm)
- Pliers—needle nose, round nose
- Earring hooks

Light as air, or rather as a feather, these lovely earrings are as fun to make as they are to wear. A little tape, a bit of wire, and a touch of fancy cutting are all you need! Not keen on wearing earrings made of tape? Washi tape feathers also make great gift toppers. If you won't be using them for earrings, you can (but don't have to) skip the wire.

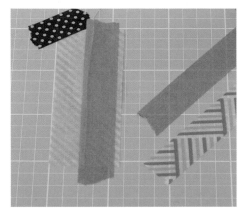

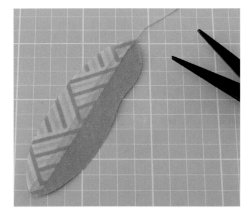

1. Cut a piece of wide 1¼ in. (30 mm) washi tape approximately 3 in. (7.5 cm) long. Place it on your work surface with the sticky side facing up. It may help to use two small strips of tape to secure it. Cut a piece of wire approximately 5 in. (12.5 cm) long. Place the wire in the center of the tape.

2. Cut a piece of standard ⅝ in. (15 mm) washi tape approximately 3 in. (7.5 cm) long. Place it on top of the wide tape so that the left edge slightly overlaps the wire. Repeat with a second piece of tape on the opposite side.

3. You will now have a tape rectangle with a wire sandwiched inside and about 2 in. (5 cm) of wire hanging out one side. The side with the wire will be the bottom of your feather and the top of the earring. Cut the tape into the shape of a feather, being careful not to cut the wire.

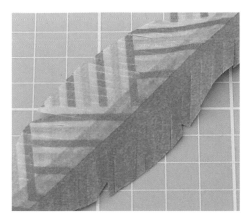

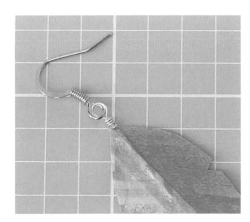

4. Create small parallel cuts all the way up and down the sides of the feather. Cut out a few notches on each side to create a more realistic feather shape.

5. Using your pliers, form a small loop at the top of the feather about ⅛ in. (3 mm) from where the tape ends. Attach the earring hook, and then wrap the end of the wire around the straight piece of wire between the feather and the loop. Cut off the excess wire.

PLAY TIME

Have some fun with your collection of tapes and a whole lot of imagination. These playful projects are perfect to do with or for kids (or for the young at heart). You can create masks, mobiles, and crowns, make stickers, try doodling with tape, or go big by making a wall mural— no paint required!

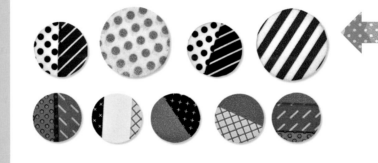

Quick Starts

There's far more fun to be had when you think beyond the strip. Turn your favorite tape into stickers or use it to enhance your doodles with color and pattern. These quick ideas are a great jumping-off point for dreaming up your own creations.

Washi Tape Dots

These playful stickers are a welcome addition to all sorts of projects. Try using them to create pictures and patterns or for your favorite crafts (see page 11).

Specialty Stickers

Why add a simple strip when you could add a bow, a flower, or a cat? Specialty rolls of tape with individual pictures are easily transformed into beautiful stickers (see page 11).

Geometric Stickers

Snip geometric stickers right off the roll. Squares, triangles, and diamonds are easy to cut—no special tricks required. They make great accents for any craft project; alternatively, use the shapes to build patterns and pictures.

Colorful Doodle

Color in the blank spaces of your drawings with washi tape shapes. For the perfect fit, use a craft knife and gently peel off bits of tape.

Start with the Tape

Apply short strips of tape to a piece of paper. Use your imagination to transform them into whatever you please. Make sure to use a ballpoint pen or fine permanent marker when drawing on the tape.

Draw with Tape

Forget the pen—use washi tape strips and shapes to create pictures. Build pictures using simple shapes or use the parchment paper sticker method (see page 10) to create more ornate shapes.

Classic Crowns

Who hasn't wanted to be Queen (or King) for the day? A washi tape crown is a wonderful way to add an air of ceremony to your celebration.

You will need:

- 28 x 22 in. (71 x 56 cm) poster board
- Crown template on page 124 (if desired)
- Ruler
- Pen or pencil
- Scissors
- Washi tape
- Stapler

Tip: When making a classic crown shape, cut your first triangle out and then use it as a template for cutting the rest. This will help you to keep the shape consistent.

1. Along the long side of your poster board, measure 6 in. (15 cm) up from the bottom. Mark at a few points, then cut. Wrap your 6-in. (15-cm) deep piece of poster board around the head of the child (or adult). You want it to be about 2 in. (5 cm) longer than the circumference of the head. Cut off any excess.

2. Decorate the flat crown with washi tape. Try diagonal stripes, horizontal stripes, geometric patterns, or confetti triangles. The more tape you add, the more dynamic the finished crown will be.

3. Once you've finished decorating, cut the top edge of the poster board into a crown shape. You can either do this freehand or first flip the crown over and draw the desired shape on the back before cutting.

4. Wrap the crown around the wearer's head, holding the ends together at the correct size. Remove from the head and staple a couple of times to secure the ends.

Rainbow Necklaces

Colorful paper necklaces are as fun to make as they are to wear. This cheerful project features two styles of washi tape beads in all the colors of the rainbow. When stringing beads, it can help to wrap a piece of tape around the string end for a makeshift needle.

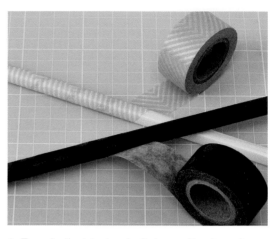

1. To make the tube beads, first cover the straws in washi tape. Starting at one end, wrap the tape around the straw on the diagonal, making sure that the tape lines up but doesn't overlap. Continue wrapping until the entire straw is covered.

3. Next, make the flat beads. Cover both sides of a piece of card stock in washi tape. You want to cover as much of the paper with tape as possible—stripes and collage strips are both great for this.

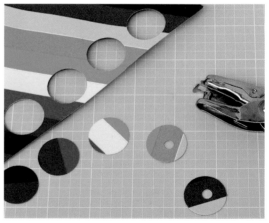

4. Punch circles out of the washi tape-covered card stock with the circle punch. Then, punch a hole in the center of each circle with the hole punch.

You will need:
- Colorful plastic straws
- Washi tape
- Scissors
- Card stock
- 1-in. (2.5-cm) circle punch
- Standard hole punch
- String

2. Cut the covered straws into 1-in. (2.5-cm) sections.

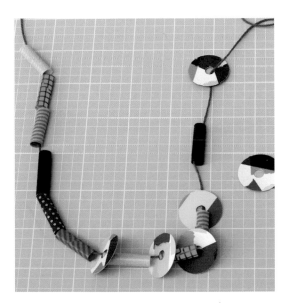

5. String your beads together to make a necklace. Make sure you tie one end of the string to a bead so that all the beads don't slide off when you move it. Once the necklace is complete, tie the ends together.

Fancy Cat Stick Puppets

Craft up a cluster of adorable cat puppets to play with or to admire. Washi tape stripes and a sweet heart-shaped nose ensure these kitties are of the friendly variety. Making these puppets is the perfect rainy-day activity for you and your young friends—and at the end you get to have a puppet show!

You will need

- Card stock
- Bowl, approx 6 in. (15 cm) in diameter
- Pencil
- Eraser
- Washi tape
- Scissors
- Parchment or waxed paper
- Fine-tipped marker or ballpoint pen
- Glue (optional)
- Wooden craft stick

Once you've mastered the art of the washi tape cat, why not try creating different creatures? I'd love to see your creations—tweet me pictures of your washi tape puppets: @marisaedghill

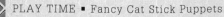

1. With a pencil, lightly draw around the outside of your bowl on the card stock. At the top of the circle, sketch two pointed cat ear shapes. Erase the line between the ears and the head.

2. Cover the ear shapes with washi tape. Try to line up the pattern where possible. Next add washi tape stripes for whiskers and fur markings. Apply three stripes to each cheek and the forehead.

3. With a pair of scissors, cut out the puppet shape. Try to cut slightly on the inside of the pencil line for a cleaner look.

4. Create the nose and eyes of your cat by applying strips of washi tape to parchment or waxed paper and then cutting out the desired shapes. To make the heart-shaped nose, fold washi tape-covered parchment in half and then cut half a heart shape. Draw on the mouth, whiskers, eye, and ear details.

5. Apply strips of washi tape to a leftover piece of card stock. Cut out a bow shape. Glue or tape it to your cat puppet.

6. Decorate a wooden craft stick with a few strips of washi tape. Tape the stick to the back of your puppet.

Add a little bit of extra glamour to your mask with a flower made out of three tape-covered circles or a cluster of pretty washi tape feathers. Learn how to make feathers on page 106.

You will need:

- Paper mask
- Hole punch
- Washi tape
- Scissors
- Craft knife
- Elastic

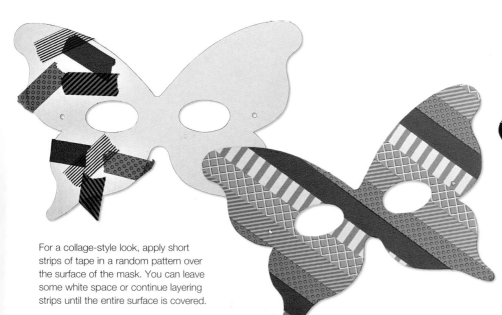

Carnival Masks

In the mood for a bit of make believe? Plain paper masks from your local craft store are transformed into works of wearable art with a handful of colorful washi tapes. This pretty project is perfect for birthday parties, play dates, or even impromptu masquerade balls.

1. Start with a plain paper mask in your desired shape. Punch out the holes for the elastic, but don't connect it just yet.

2. Apply stripes of washi tape in a few different colors and designs, alternating designs to create a pattern. Once the entire surface of the mask is covered, trim the tape ends from around the outside of the mask with a pair of scissors. Alternatively, you can simply fold the tape ends around to the back of the mask.

3. Flip the mask over and cut the tape from inside the eyeholes with a craft knife. Cutting around the edges and eyeholes of the mask can be a bit tricky. It's best if an adult does this step!

4. Once your mask is fully decorated, use a pen or a craft knife to reopen the holes for the string and connect the elastic to your mask.

For a collage-style look, apply short strips of tape in a random pattern over the surface of the mask. You can leave some white space or continue layering strips until the entire surface is covered.

Make a Mural

Add some personality to blank walls with a washi tape mural. Makes a wonderful afternoon activity to do with kids or try creating one for playrooms or parties. Get bored easily? Once you're ready to make a new washi tape world, simply peel off the tape and start afresh.

Tip: While washi tape is generally safe on most surfaces, if your paint is older, a bit flaky, or your walls have many layers of paint, it might pull off paint when you remove it. It's always a good idea to do a test strip before committing to a full mural.

1. To create your own washi tape garden, apply evenly spaced stems to the wall. Leave 10–12 in. (25–30 cm) between each tape strip.

2. For a simple starburst-style flower, cut eight pieces of tape each about 6 in. (15 cm) long (2a). Place two strips above the stem, intersecting at a 90-degree angle (2b). Continue adding intersecting strips until the flower is formed (2c).

3. For an 8-petal flower, cut four pieces of tape each about 8-in. (20-cm) long. Place the first two strips above the stem so that they intersect at a 90-degree angle. Apply the other two strips in the spaces between. Shape each petal with three short pieces of tape.

4. You can add more details to your flowers with slim tape strips placed in the middle of the petals to resemble stamens and large washi tape dots for the centers.

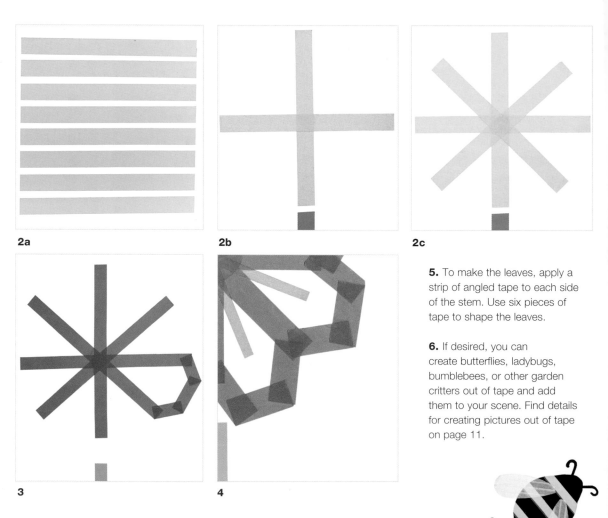

2a

2b

2c

3

4

5. To make the leaves, apply a strip of angled tape to each side of the stem. Use six pieces of tape to shape the leaves.

6. If desired, you can create butterflies, ladybugs, bumblebees, or other garden critters out of tape and add them to your scene. Find details for creating pictures out of tape on page 11.

6

When drawing on walls with washi tape, you can either create as you go, building a freeform picture, or plan your picture by first sketching it out and then transferring your vision onto the wall. Either way, you'll be sure to love the result.

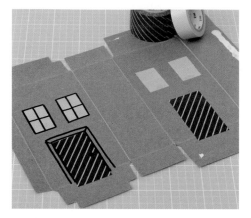

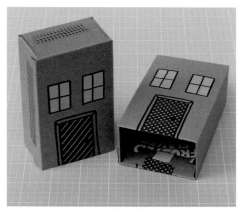

1. Carefully open the box at the seam and unfold. Place the flattened box, printed side down, on your work surface. Add washi tape doors and windows. If desired, use a fine-tipped marker to draw on extra details.

2. Refold the box into its original shape with washi tape decoration on the outside. Use glue or tape to secure the top and side seams. To help your house stand firm, fold the bottom flaps inward and use tape or glue to hold them in place.

3. To create the roof, take a second box the same size as the first. Turn the box inside out, securing the seams with tape or glue. Measure the top edge of the box. Mark the same length on the side edge and draw a line between the two points. Repeat on the back of the box. Draw connecting lines on the sides of the box.

Upcycled Box Village

Transform small boxes into a village of adorable cottages perfect for an afternoon of make believe. Colorful roofs and welcoming washi tape doors make these wee houses a delight to construct. Once you've founded your tape town, it's sure to inspire hours of imaginative play. For each house, you will need two boxes of the same size.

You will need:
- Small boxes
- Washi tape
- Scissors
- Fine-tipped permanent marker (optional)
- Glue
- Craft knife

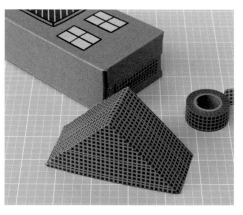

5. Cover all sides of the roof with strips of washi tape. Trim the loose tape ends with scissors. Place the roof on top of the house.

4. Use a craft knife to cut along the lines.

Why not create a city map on the floor or a large piece of poster board? Set your sweet houses up along the streets and you've got a wonderful washi tape world to play in!

Tip: Individual cereal or pudding mix boxes are the perfect size for creating your village.

Under The Sea Mobile

A simple mobile in soothing shades of blue makes a lovely accent for a kid's room, nursery, or as a gift for your favorite sea-lover. Not a big fan of fish? No need to avoid this project—simply switch out the fish for a shape you prefer.

You will need:

- 6 in. (15 cm) embroidery hoop
- Washi tape
- Scissors
- Card stock
- Pen or marker
- Fish template (see page 124)
- 1 in. (2.5 cm) circle punch
- Small hole punch
- String or twine
- Wooden beads

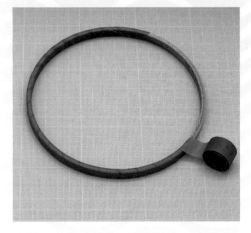

1. Open the embroidery hoop and remove the inner hoop. Cover the inner hoop with washi tape by wrapping the tape around on the diagonal.

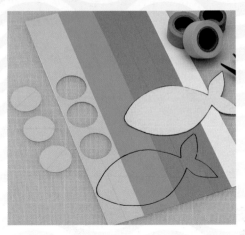

2. Cover both sides of a piece of card stock with washi tape. Trace around the fish template and cut out. Punch nine circles of tape-covered card with the circle punch.

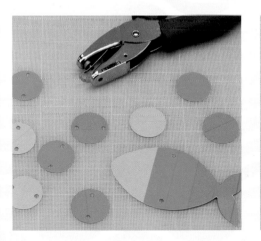

3. Punch holes at the top and bottom of the fish shape and each circle with the small hole punch.

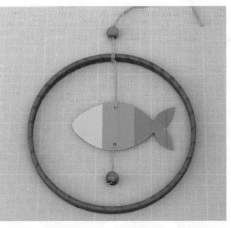

4. Cut a piece of twine approximately 18 in. (45 cm) long. Tie a wooden bead onto one end. String the fish shape onto the twine above the bead. Tie onto the top of the hoop, wrapping it around a couple of times, so that the fish hangs in the center of the hoop. Tie extra twine into a loop at the top of the hoop. Cut off any excess and hide the knot inside a bead.

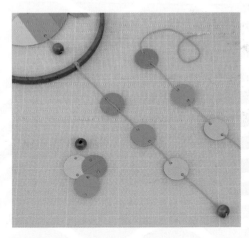

5. Cut three pieces of twine, approximately 12 in. (30 cm) long. Tie a bead at one end, then string three circle shapes onto each piece. To make the beads and shapes easier to thread, wrap a piece of tape around the string end, and snip it off when you have finished. Attach to the bottom of the hoop, ensuring that they are spaced evenly.

Templates

These templates are shown at actual size.
All you need to do is trace them off and
follow the instructions on the relevant
project page listed.

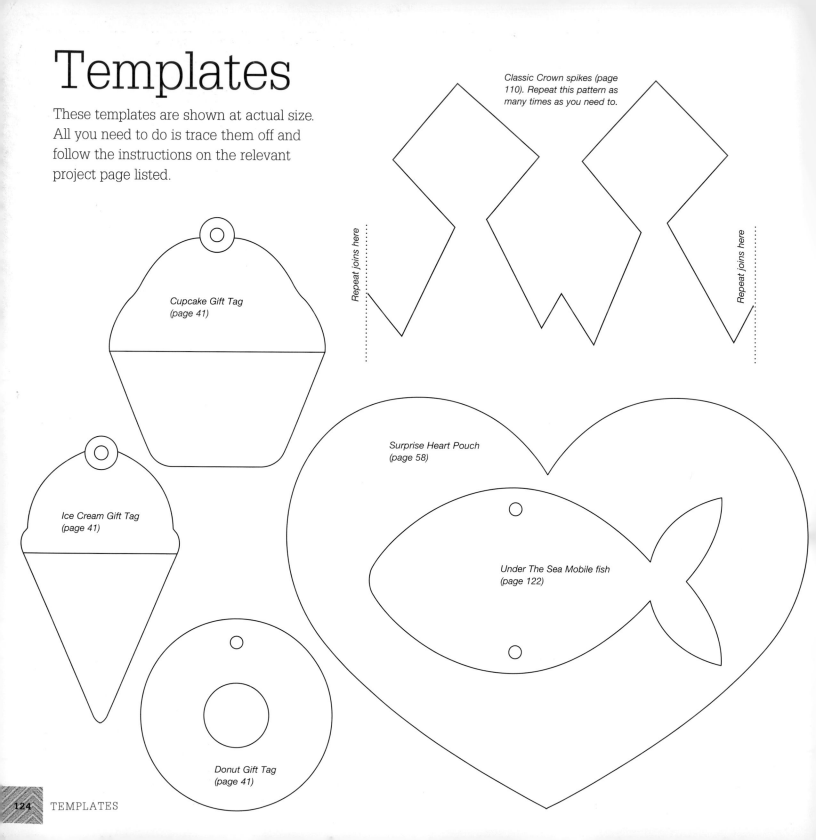

Classic Crown spikes (page 110). Repeat this pattern as many times as you need to.

Repeat joins here

Repeat joins here

Cupcake Gift Tag (page 41)

Ice Cream Gift Tag (page 41)

Surprise Heart Pouch (page 58)

Under The Sea Mobile fish (page 122)

Donut Gift Tag (page 41)

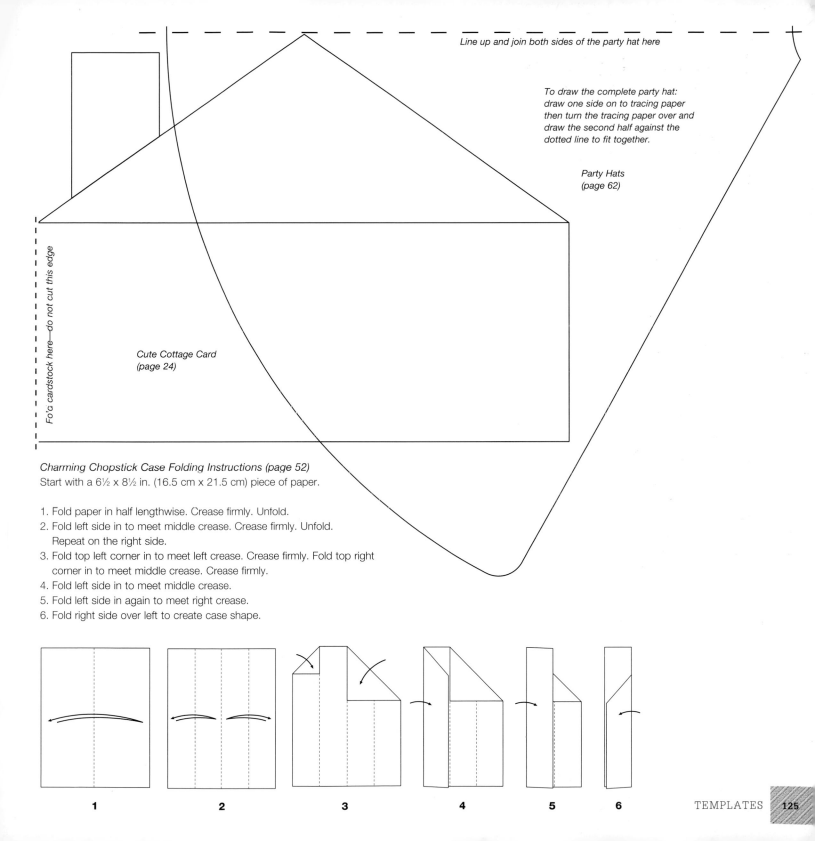

Line up and join both sides of the party hat here

*To draw the complete party hat:
draw one side on to tracing paper
then turn the tracing paper over and
draw the second half against the
dotted line to fit together.*

*Party Hats
(page 62)*

Fo'a cardstock here—do not cut this edge

*Cute Cottage Card
(page 24)*

Charming Chopstick Case Folding Instructions (page 52)
Start with a 6½ x 8½ in. (16.5 cm x 21.5 cm) piece of paper.

1. Fold paper in half lengthwise. Crease firmly. Unfold.
2. Fold left side in to meet middle crease. Crease firmly. Unfold.
   Repeat on the right side.
3. Fold top left corner in to meet left crease. Crease firmly. Fold top right
   corner in to meet middle crease. Crease firmly.
4. Fold left side in to meet middle crease.
5. Fold left side in again to meet right crease.
6. Fold right side over left to create case shape.

1   **2**   **3**   **4**   **5**   **6**

Index

Credits

Quarto would like to thank the following supplier for contributing their washi tape to the book:

MAKING IS FUN!

mt
masking tape

Kamoi Kakoshi Co., Ltd
236 Katashima-cho
Kurashiki-shi
Okayama Pref.
710-8611
Japan

Thank you also to Blaíthín and Oisín for being such great models.

Images courtesy of shutterstock.com and the following photographers: adpePhoto, page 71; Africa Studio, page 119 (main); Macrovector, page 119 (left); sutsaiy, page 119 (center, top); Vasilyev Alexandr, page 119 (center, bottom); grmarc, page 119 (right, top); StevanZZ, page 119 (center, bottom).

All step-by-step and other images are the copyright of Quarto Publishing plc. While every effort has been made to credit contributors, Quarto would like to apologize should there have been any omissions or errors—and would be pleased to make the appropriate correction for future editions of the book.

Author's acknowledgements

Thank you to the team at Quarto, notably Karin Skånberg, Nicki Dowey, and Phil Wilkins, for transforming a giant box of crafts into this beautiful book. Huge thanks to Chelsea Edwards and Jackie Palmer for their guidance and expertise all along the way. And a special thank you to my husband Elias for his unwavering support and patience even while I covered every surface of the house with tape!